Praise For This Bo

"Houston, we have a problem."

Well, I feel like I'm on that spaceship, because I have a problem.

Got you interested?

My problem: I don't know if I have enough words in my vocabulary to tell the world about your book.

Put most simply, this is the best guide to success that I believe has ever been written, not just for insurance agency folks, but for anyone in business of any kind - small or large, hometown or national, owner or staff member.

My solution: I am going to write my thoughts, probably not in a logical order, but together making the point above.

The first of 14 books I have written in my 60+ year career of working with independent insurance agencies was "Insurance Agency Advertising and Public Relations," published in 1963, 56 years ago. It was the first book ever written on the subject.

After I read Eddie's book, I took a long look at my initial work, and drew one conclusion: The marketing concepts I was able to illustrate back then, were very much the same as what good marketing looks and feels like now. Of course, communications methods, tools, et al, have hugely advanced in those years. But conceptually, they are very similar.

I was even more excited that this part of the book was able to bring together the theories of marketing; but even better, organize them so that they clearly extoll an ideal step-by-step action plan that makes all the philosophy come into reality.

Yet marketing via a planned approach, even using the step-by-step map that this book provides is, in itself, not enough.

Without understanding the basics of finance, leadership, sales, customer service and human resources, the insurance agency owner wouldn't attain the success levels that Eddie Price (and many other agency owners I have known) have reached.

And the fact that he has removed the smoke and mirrors that often surround the suggested action steps in many "how to" books is a major attraction of this work. "Gut level" wording comes to mind. He pulls no punches and doesn't waste time and effort giving easy solutions to the basic facts of agency management life.

My conclusion - "He tells it like it is," keeps coming to mind.

The book was written (and helps keep us involved) with the idea that he is explaining business life in general to his daughter, Jenna.

With a form of "tongue in cheek" sincerity, Eddie also brings in just enough humor to constantly add to the interest level.

I plan to publicize the book in every way possible. I am going to recommend to my 50,000+ mailing list of agencies that this book needs to be in the possession of every single person in their shop. The book needs to be a "must read" for every new employee.

One of the dangers of the book is that the reader gets so involved he or she just keeps going until it is finished! My recommendation is that you instruct your staff members to read one chapter at a time.

Here's a better idea: Get the book for each member of your staff; then, open your weekly meetings with a discussion of that week's featured chapter/subject. When everybody boosts, everybody wins.

My last point about this wonderful work is that it could well be too limited. Looking back at it now, chapter by chapter, I realize that every bit of it applies to ANY business. I hope that the word can get out about it to the rest of the business world. Although written for insurance folks, this book could well be the primer for practically any person in any business. No kidding…..I meant every word above.

George Nordhaus
Founder and Chairman, USA Insurance Network

The Perfect Insurance Agency

The Perfect Insurance Agency
Simple Changes to Ensure Success

Eddie Price

The Perfect Insurance Agency
Simple Changes to Ensure Success

ISBN-13: 978-0-578-48575-1

Cover design by Luisito C. Pangilinan

Jenesis Software, Inc.
307 Georgetowne Drive
Elon, NC 27244
United States

www.JenesisSoftware.com

After reading the book, The Perfect Insurance Agency, Eddie Price has gifted not only his daughter Jenna, but anyone who reads this rendition of how to better run their business. This heartfelt book is not only filled with advice on how best to succeed in business, but includes many of life's principals that if applied, would make any individual or business become better. As I read the book, I could hear Eddie's voice, and envisioned his body language as if he were telling the story of his life as an entrepreneur. Moreover, this book is so heart touching because it was written for Eddie's greatest source of pride, his daughter Jenna. As a Father of twin daughters, I related very well with the emotions that Eddie poured into his writing as he spelled out these life lessons to his little girl, who has grown up to be a wonderful young woman. Having known Eddie since 1998, I've witnessed him practice what he has written in this book, and the advice he has so lovingly passed along to his daughter.

Marty Karriker
President
Charlotte Insurance

"The Perfect Insurance Agency" is an inspiration to anyone who values not only business success but personal growth and achievement. The practices within this book have inspired me to review my approach to life, business colleagues and personal relationships. A "Must Have" for everyone - not just insurance agencies!

Kim Vaughn
Planning & Logistics Manager
ZINK Holdings LLC

About the Author

Eddie Price graduated from the University of North Carolina at Chapel Hill in 1988 and began his career in the insurance industry as an agent for North Carolina Farm Bureau Insurance Company. In 1991, Eddie started Carolina Insurance, an independent insurance agency, from scratch. Later he went back to school to learn computer programming and with that new knowledge, created automation for his agency. By the late 90s, he began receiving inquiries from other agencies who had heard about his software. So, inadvertently, he began to sell the system to others. He named the product Jenesis, and the company Jenesis Software, after his then five-year-old daughter, Jenna.

Both businesses continued to grow over the years. In January 2018, Eddie made the difficult decision to sell his first baby, Carolina Insurance and focus only on Jenesis Software.

During his 27 years as an agency owner, while Eddie successfully acquired and sold several agencies, he continued to learn the most from the agencies through his Jenesis relationships.

Dedication

To my wife, Lisa, who allows me to be the obsessive compulsive person I am. I know it's not easy living with someone who also has the next big life project underway as soon as the last one is complete. Without you by my side, and I mean that literally, every day, and I meat that literally too, my energy and passion would be completely deflated. Thank you for the fun we have, the daily hugs and constant positive attitude, and thank you for allowing me to be me ☺

To my daughter, Jenna, you have been such an inspiration for so much I have done in life. From naming my company, Jenesis, after you to this book being about our conversations, you have influenced much of my success. Thanks for being kind to others and for at least making me think you are proud of me. Working to make you proud has had many benefits.

To my mom and dad, who not only gave me life, but also showed me how to live it. You were the perfect parents and I miss you both every day.

Table of Contents

Foreword

Eddie's book is masterful and a must read not just for insurance industry members or business owners but anyone and everyone who runs a business and wants to succeed. He had my attention and interest from the very beginning and he kept it throughout every chapter. Even though some of his points, topics and messages might have been around for many years, his approach to them is unique, entertaining yet thought provoking.

As a global speaker and an international bestselling author, and an avid reader for more than fifty years (I have read on average one to two books every week my entire life), I do have in my own world the right to comment on his great book. I can tell without hesitation, if I had had the opportunity to read this book early in my career I would have achieved even more than I have both faster and easier.

I don't like long introductions or a lot of—blah, blah, blah stuff —in the beginning of books and since Eddie asked me to write this I'm going to honor my approach to my writing.

If you don't buy and devour every page of this book you will never know what you could have accomplished. But, I will guarantee if you do and you apply his techniques, ideas and approaches, the time and effort will be nothing compared tom the results you will achieve.

Thank you Eddie for a great contribution to the "International Self-Help Library" of the world's greatest books. (I just made that up but I believe it's appropriate).

Seriously, I will close this with one of my life's greatest mentor's—Charlie "Tremendous" Jones (rest in peace Charlie) —favorite lines: *"Five years from today you will be the same person you are today except for the people you meet and the books you read."*

Tim Connor
Global Speaker and Bestselling Author

Acknowledgement

I want to start by thanking Dr. John Estrella, whom without; this book would have not been possible. John helps so many realize their dreams and is always so positive and caring.

I also want to thank those how helped by reading my manuscript and providing feedback. They include but are not limited to Lisa Price, Jenna Price, Ryan Bowman, Christy Alaimo, Amy Presley, Kim Vaughn, Phil Price, Amy Sherrill, and Donna Gentry.

INTRODUCTION

This book chronicles the dinner conversations that he had with his daughter, Jenna, who wisely followed in his footsteps. He wants her to be successful and to do so in a shorter period of time with less pain. He shared all the struggles and challenges that he encountered along the way. He gave her tips on what to expect, how to react to certain situations, and most importantly, how to make the process fun and rewarding.

CHAPTER **1**

OVERVIEW

"I find that the harder I work, the more luck I seem to have."
—Thomas Jefferson

"Try not to become a person of success. Rather become a person of value."
—Albert Einstein

"Stop chasing the money and start chasing the passion."
—Tony Hsieh

"Success is not the key to happiness. Happiness is the key to success. If you love what you are doing, you will be successful."
—Albert Schweitzer

"The only place where success comes before work is in the dictionary."
—Vidal Sassoon

My Dear Jenna,

It seems like only yesterday when I finished college and I began the journey of work and life as an adult.

I want to teach you some of the things I learned along the way. Don't get me wrong, I don't know everything. As a matter of fact, I don't really know what I don't know. But, I have learned many things over the last 30 years and many of those lessons I learned the hard way, by trial and error. I believe passing what I have learned on to you will help you in your future. My intent here is to help you live a happy, fulfilling life by deciding what it is that will make you happy and then learning strategies that will help you get what you want.

Looking back, the phrase that I've learned over the years, "you don't know what you don't know," would not have made any sense to me back then. But it makes a lot of sense now! You really don't know what you don't know. If this doesn't click with you, give it some thought and remember it as you experience learning over the course of your life and career.

My Beginning

After I finished college I took a job as an insurance agent with a direct writer, Farm Bureau. When I left the position a few years later to be an entrepreneur and open my own agency, I already knew how to be an insurance agent. I was excited about the possibility of being an entrepreneur and business owner. It was pretty easy finding an office location to rent, buying computers, and doing some simple advertising. Even getting a few appointments with carriers wasn't too hard thanks to my experience with Farm Bureau.

So, I began the journey. Going into work every morning, I knew that one day I was going to have more people working with me. I was building a business.

Each day I would open up, answer the phones, quote, do some prospecting, make decisions about advertising along the way and before I knew it, every month was a little better than the one before. Even though I wasn't making as much as I wanted to financially, I believed my future was bright. It was time. I was ready to hire my first employee.

Hiring my first agent caused my income to decrease because I had to pay them mostly from what I was taking home. Then, we both began the process that I'd begun earlier of climbing a ladder, building the book of business. It became difficult for the two of us to keep up with things so it was time for me to hire a second employee.

I think you can probably see where this is going. When I hired the second employee, the first employee obviously didn't want to take a cut in pay to help with the new hire, so I reduced my income to pay for the new agent. The three of us then began the process, once again, of building back to where we were before in terms of profit and my income.

I'm not going to keep telling you the story over and over as it continues to build. I'm sure you get the point.

Somewhere along the way, an employee left me. I had to regroup, punt, and start over with hiring and replacing the agent that left.

Shortly following, a few customers started to complain that they were not getting as good of service as they got from me.

Everything had gone so well up to this point. But now, I was a little bummed an employee left me and the other employee wasn't as loved by my customers. I began to wonder what had I done wrong. Where had I failed?

If that wasn't bad enough, once I figured out how to move forward in a more profitable and structured way, I had the next big lesson in front of me. What I didn't realize when I started out was this. Let's say your agency writes a hundred policies a month for example. When you started your agency, you obviously grow by 100% that first year. If you could keep that pace up and never lose a customer you would grow by 100% in year two, 50% in year three, 33%, in year four and slowly reduce the growth percentage of the next 20 years to the point you are growing my single digits each year. Now, let's add some reality to the example. Let's say you lose ten percent of your customers each year. People of course pass on, move, sell what they have been insuring with you, and sometimes even move their business to another agency. Now, while adding twelve hundred new policies each year and losing ten percent of your customer base, you will grow by 90% in year two, 43% in year three, 27% in year four, 19% in year five and by year ten your growth will be in the single digits, pretty much flat.

So, after the first few years of being in business, and getting a little better at leadership, finances, customer service and so on, I started to realize the growth I had experienced every year, for so many years, was starting to level off.

Well, Jenna, I'm going to attempt to give you the lessons I've learned over the last 30 years. I hope that you can take these lessons, apply them, add to them from your own experience, and continue to evolve creating a business and not just a job. I want to help you learn how to work on your business and not just in your business. I will teach you how to play a strategic game of chess and not just to play tennis where you're running from one side of the court to the other every time the ball goes somewhere you're not.

I'm not going to teach you more about insurance. Most agency owners are really good at product knowledge. I am going to spend more time telling you what I've learned about marketing, sales, and especially what I've learned about leadership, people, and self-improvement. Let's get started.

Can you pass the "one-month-off" test"?

One thing we're going to try to accomplish as we think about your future is the "one-month-off" test. If you can take one month off of work, and your business continues to run well, then you have successfully created a sustainable company that can thrive without you.

Morning routines

Let's start at the beginning of your day. It's important to start the day off right. Have you heard the saying about getting up on the right side of the bed? I think it's more important to get up on the right side of the head. In other words, start your day with positive thoughts.

If you research morning routines of successful people, you will see that most are simple and that most are very similar. For example, most promote starting the day by drinking a glass of cold water, taking a cold shower, meditation time, or exercise.

I do all of these some days, none of them some days, and some of them most days. You need to come up with a consistent morning routine and stick to it most of the time. I am a big believer that you should not set your alarm clock, hit snooze a few times, then roll out of bed and into the shower, then out the door to go to work. We need a little time to get set for a successful day. My advice is to research what others do and come up with your plan. Start simple and change over time to figure out what works best for you.

How much should you work?

When I was in my late twenties, my dad introduced me to a friend of his, a doctor he had admired for years. My dad told the doctor that I was very successful and I worked all the time. My dad felt that successful people worked more than unsuccessful people and that if you worked 50, 60, 70, or 80 hours a week, you would be successful.

Here is the funny part about that conversation with the doctor. When my dad said "Eddie works all the time", the doctor, in a very polite, curious, and sincere way responded: "Why?"

You see, that that guy, he did not eqate more hours worked to being more successful as much as he did what you were doing when you worked. I imagine he may have wondered why this young guys had to put in so many hours to get things done.

My point here is to tell you that you need to put effort into anything you want to do well, but if you put all your effort into one thing, what happens to the other important things in life like relationships, health, and your spiritual well-being?

The key to success is putting the right amount of effort into the right areas of your life, consistently.

What will you do with your 24 hours each day?

You should sleep 8 hours so that leaves you 16. If you work around 8 hours a day, that leaves you 8. You should exercise most days and let's say that takes an hour of your time, you are still left with 7. You should spend time with friends and family. Some of that can be done on weekends but let's say you want to spend 2-3 quality hours daily with friends or family, you are still left with 4-5 hours every day to meditate, relax, read, and improve.

Where are you going?

Let's start by deciding where you want to go. Define and get clarity on your personal, professional, and financial goals. Visualize it. If you don't know where you want to go, and how things will look when you get there, there is no way to plan the journey that will allow you to arrive where you want to be.

Most people use the word goals when they discuss plans for the future. I would like for you to use **WHY-SMART** goals. Let's talk about what this means.

W - Written
H - Harmonious
Y - Your

S - Specific
M - Measurable
A - Achievable
R - Relevant
T - Time-based

Let me start by saying that **WHY-SMART** is a framework for how to structure goals that are more likely to be achieved.

Let's start with W which stands for Written. It is very important for you to write your goals down. Many studies have shown that goals that are written are more likely to be achieved than goals unwritten.

H is for Harmonious. Your goals need to be in harmony with your values and beliefs. If you had a goal that went against your values, for example, it would be very difficult to do what it takes to accomplish that goal.

The Y stands for Your. These goals need to be your goals. If someone else tells you what your goals are you will not have the passion to be able to do what it takes to accomplish the goals. Especially remember this as a leader, if you inflict goals on your team, they are less likely to accomplish those goals than if you work with them to establish goals that they believe in and that are important to them.

The S is for Specific. If I have a goal to lose weight, but I don't decide how much I'm going to weigh or how many pounds I'm going to lose, how will I ever know if I reach the goal?

The M stands for Measurable. Again, if my goal is to lose weight, in order to measure it, I have to use some criteria that is measurable. For example, I can measure weighing a specific weight or losing a specific number of pounds, but to say, just to lose weight or just to get in better shape is not specific or measurable.

The letter A is for Achievable. It would be foolish to set a goal that was so extreme it could never be reached and therefore you would never make a true effort. I do want to mention here however, I like to think of A as also representing the word ambitious. Studies have shown that people who set more challenging goals reach greater successes than those who set lower goals. That does not mean they reach their goals more than the other people, it just means that the level of achievement is greater, when the goal is greater.

The R stands for Relevant. If you have a goal that is not relevant to your desired outcomes but it makes sense for the path that you are on, you will have less passion to be motivated to do what it takes to achieve the goal.

Last but certainly not least, is T, which stands for Time-based. If we go back to the weight loss goal, if my goal is to lose 10 pounds, but I don't know when I plan for that to happen, how can that be measurable? But if my goal is to lose 10 pounds by March 15th of a specific year, when that day gets here, assuming I documented my weight at the beginning of this process, I will know exactly, and be able to measure exactly, how many pounds are lost, or possibly gained.

So that's it, Jenna. We would like to start by creating one, two, or possibly three goals using the WHY-SMART framework for our personal, professional, and financial objectives. It's important to not have too many goals or it will be unlikely we will be able to accomplish any of them.

How will you get there?

Now that we have established our WHY-SMART goals, it's time to create a plan for achieving those goals. This is where action steps come into play. Each goal will have one or more action steps which are required to reach the goal. For my weight loss goal, in order to lose 10 lbs by March 15th of a specific year, I might need one action step that says I need to log my food into an app so I make sure I'm not going over the correct calorie count each day. I may have another action step that says I need to exercise 30 minutes each day 6 days a week. Also, these action steps should be time-based and measurable.

Something else I want to mention while we are talking about how to reach goals is that I believe it is very important to always be learning. We learn in different ways, like reading, spending time with mentors, taking classes, trial, and error, etc. Just remember that the most expensive and slowest way to learn is trial and error.

I believe that we all should read or listen to audiobooks if that's easier for you. If that's not something that happens naturally for you, and it doesn't for many people, this could be one of your goals. Your goal could be to read one book a month and your action steps could be things like reading 10 pages a day, for example.

I've heard it said that readers are leaders, and leaders are readers. Too many people stop reading about things like health and fitness, marriage, relationships, and business because they feel like they have a lot of experience in that area, and they know quite a bit. The problem is like I said earlier, we don't know, what we don't know.

I also want to mention to you the importance of focus. I think it's funny that sometimes I think to myself, I really need to focus on a lot of things this week. Isn't that hilarious? To focus on many things!

How crazy is that? Multitasking doesn't work! Many studies prove, beyond the shadow of a doubt, that multitasking extends the time it takes to accomplish any given task and reduces the quality of all. Don't get me wrong, I have tried it many times, and I'm embarrassed to say I still find myself doing it today.

The only difference between people who are more successful and the people who are less successful is not the hours in the day, and is not usually a result of luck or intelligence. The only difference is it's primarily that successful people choose to do the right things most of the time. What we choose to do each and every day impacts our results. Not to mention the fact that when we focus on a few key tasks, we do them better and reduce stress in our lives tremendously.

In his book, The 80/20 Principle, Richard Koch explains what the 80/20 principle is and how we can use it to improve our lives.

The 80/20 principle basically says that we wear 20% of our clothes 80% of the time, we walk on 20% of our carpet 80% of the time, 80% of the beer in the world is consumed by 20% of the beer drinkers, 80% of a company's profits come from 20% of its customers, 80% of a company's complaints come from 20% of its customers, and so on.

So, why is this important? If we can identify the 20% of what we do with our time that is currently giving us 80% of the results that we like, then we can analyze the other 80% of what we're doing, and start to eliminate or reduce those activities. For example, of all the time you spend with friends, you probably get 80% of your happiness from 20% of those friends. So, spend more time with those 20%, and less time with the 80%. If 20% of what you do at work results in 80% of your accomplishments, figure out what you're doing 80% of the time that's getting you only 20% of the results and start eliminating, delegating, or reducing those tasks.

This brings up a good point. We have heard that it's important to do the right thing. Well, I think this holds two meanings. One is that we should always do the ethical and moral thing. The other is that we need to choose the right thing as it pertains to the most important thing. There's just not enough hours in the day to do EVERYTHING we may want to do or that others recommend or ask us to do. Be wise in your choices.

I have mostly done the right thing as it pertains to ethics. When I was in my early twenties and just starting my agency, I came up with something I told customers that help me a lot. Back then, you could write someone's insurance and backdate the effective date because the applications were on paper that you mailed to the carrier. Also, you could take a payment and because you had to mail the payment to the carrier, you could date the payment on a date earlier than they actually paid. I would often be asked by my customers if I could backdate the application so they would avoid a lapse in coverage or backdate the payment date so they would avoid cancellation. This in some ways seemed harmless. However, it was still a lie. Is it ok to lie if it doesn't hurt anyone? I remember giving this a little thought and quickly decided I would not lie. So, here is what I started telling my customers. I would say, "I am so sorry, but I just can't lie to the company, I hope you understand. The good news Mr. Customer is that you know I am not one who will lie or do anything wrong. So, you know that I will always be honest with you and always do the right thing." I don't remember ever having a problem with a customer over this. If I did, I would be ok with it because I knew I did the right thing.

The law of attraction

The law of attraction says that what you think about is what you attract into your life. For example, if you think or say something like, "I hope we don't lose that big account" or "I bet Susie will forget to call Mr. Important Customer back today," then the chance of those things happening increases. A different way to speak and think would be "We sure are blessed to have that big account" or "I look forward to hearing from Susie after she talks with Mr. Important Customer today." See the difference? This may sound silly, but I have seen it work over and over. There is something about thinking and talking about things the way you want them to be rather than the way you don't want them to be, that seems to influence the outcome. Plus, there is just no downside to this behavior. It will make you, and those around you, feel better.

Find your purpose

Taking your goal setting seriously will help you find your purpose. This is huge. Can you think of someone you would call successful that does not seem to have a clear, focused purpose? Michael Jordan focused on basketball. Bill Gates focused on software. Garth Brooks focused on music. Not even just music, but "country" music. Another thing they all had in common was that they loved what they were doing. If you love what you do, you will be much better at it than if you find something that you think will make you a lot of money. Start by finding what you enjoy. What makes you happy? What is fun? If you are running an insurance agency, a software company, playing sports, or becoming a musician, there will be parts of that business that you don't love doing. Quickly identify those and outsource or hire the right people to do them. There will be times when you go through phases where you question your purpose. That's perfectly normal. I have done it a few times over the years. For me, when I take some time to pray and reflect, I seem to be recharged or pointed in what later I learned was the right direction.

Be Intentional

Jenna, you know how I often comment when someone stops at a traffic light or stop sign and they stop past the line (Don't even bring up that time I was over by an entire car length and we had to watch the traffic light through the sunroof. That was just one-time kid, so give me a break.)? I think the reason I don't like that is because it indicates a lack of attention and a lack of intention. We should exercise being intentional and aware of everything we do. Be intentional about caring for others. Be intentional about saying "please" and "thank you." Be intentional about the details of your website or the respect and love you give to your spouse. Everything we became good at is because we practiced it. That's true with walking, talking, driving, communicating, loving, caring, everything. So, practice being intentional with everything you do.

Humility

In the Bible, it speaks often about Jesus being and teaching humility. We will talk more about role models and mentors, but what better role model than Jesus? Even those who don't believe in Jesus or Christianity can't argue he is a great role model. He was very intentional with everything he did and said, using the law of attraction to get people to give up their possessions and jobs to follow him while remaining humble his entire life. Don't think that being humble means you are not confident. Jesus was very confident. Being humble doesn't mean you have to be weak. Bill Gates is a humble man but took on the United States Government in a lawsuit and won. My point is you should be kind and humble all the time with everyone.

Treat everyone with respect, kindness, and gratitude

It's easy in life to let yourself feel "better" than others. It's also easy to get too busy to take the time to show respect, kindness, and gratitude toward others. I just want to remind you that we are on this planet for a far greater purpose than to build a successful business. The most important thing in life is your relationship with others. Be intentional with your words and actions. Do and say things to make others feel good. Apply this principle to everyone. Of course, you should make those you love and care about feel good. But, also be aware of the clerk at the grocery store who rings up your purchase, the person who wants to merge in front of you on the highway, and those who are too busy to treat you with respect, kindness, and gratitude. You should extend respect, kindness and gratitude to all these people as well.

Choose work you are passionate about

If you love what you do, you will never have to work another day. The ability to achieve levels of success in anything that is considered to be above average normally requires extra effort more than extra intelligence. That's really good news for me. The hard part is that it's miserable to do something you don't like at all, let alone do more of it. So, those who have accomplished higher levels of success in sports, entertainment, business, and everything else, have had a passion for what they are doing. They love to do that task more than watch television or go to the movies. You will not be able to make yourself be passionate about something. You must find what you love and then just do that. For me, it has been business in general and especially things that involve data and planning. Jenna, you are obviously much better at sales than I have ever been so that may be your passion. That doesn't mean you can't successfully lead an organization but it may mean that for that organization to be all it can be, you will need to surround yourself with key people who are good at the things you don't enjoy doing.

Always do the right thing

It has been said that integrity is doing the right thing when nobody's watching. I agree completely. I can't imagine what it's like to be tempted to do wrong in business but I can imagine what it's like when I want three glasses of cold chocolate milk and four ice cream sandwiches and I just can't help myself. Everyone is weak about something so I am not going to judge. I am grateful that my weakness only puts extra pounds on my body and doesn't hurt others as poor business ethics can. I don't have the secret principle here other than to say that if you truly believe that doing right, even when others don't know you have, will result in a better, more peaceful life, then it's much easier to do the right thing.

I suppose we sometimes do the wrong thing because we thought it was the right thing. Most of the time, however, I believe that we do the wrong thing without knowing it's the wrong thing because we are unaware, and not because we thought it through and thought it was the right thing. My dad, your granddad, would tell me to "plug my brain in" when I made a mistake because I was not aware. So, if we will just keep our brains plugged in and believe that doing good, even when others don't know, will lead to a better life, then we should be on the right path.

Continue to learn by reading books and engaging mentors

We will discuss the importance of learning more when we talk about leadership and again when we talk about building your team. For now, I just want to mention that this is an easy thing to overlook. Where I have gotten this wrong in my career was when I had gotten so busy because of current success that I forget to invest in learning for the future. When I went back to school to study programming, then put that knowledge to use creating Jenesis, things started to take off. Then just a few years later, I was still just using my current skills and knowledge without expanding them to keep pace with advances in technology. I began to realize things were changing in technology and what I had learned just a few years earlier was not all I needed to know.

Technology is not the only discipline that changes over time, everything changes. You don't have to spend all your time learning, of course, because then you would not have any time to use your knowledge. However, you need to invest a percentage of your time to improve yourself. You may want to start with something like ten percent of your time devoted to self-improvement. This would equate to about five weeks a year, three days a month, one day a week or two hours per day. If you want to follow my rounding style math, I am basically assuming that one week out of fifty-two is about ten percent, three days out of thirty in a month is about ten percent, one day a week is rounding up just a little out of seven days, and if you are awak sixteen hours per day for seven days, ten percent of that is about two hours. The point is not to invest this exact amount of time but more to have an idea and a plan for about how much time, and on what schedule, you will need to allot for self-improvement.

What will you do when you get there?

So now we've created our goals, we've created our action steps to achieve those goals and we've discussed a few ways to improve and increase our knowledge and ability. Now take a moment and imagine you have accomplished those goals. We know what that will look like because we've established that with WHY-SMART goals. But think for a moment about how t it would feel to accomplish your goals. What will accomplishing your goals mean to you, your family, your friends, the people you work with, and the rest of the world?

Serving others

In their book, The Go Giver, by Bob Burg and John David Mann, they talk about the success that we can have and the satisfaction that we can feel not by being a go-getter, but by being a go-giver. I highly recommend the book. What I will tell you here is simply that you need to be focused, and include in your goals, ways in which you will give to others. If you give, you will receive. Also, one form of giving is serving. You should start serving now and not wait to reach your goals. Serving others and giving now, in my experience, will somehow magically be instrumental in you achieving your goals. By the way, most of us are selfish. Think about when someone takes a group picture. Who do you look for in the picture first? Yourself right? Not only that, if you look good in the picture, you will probably say something like, "that's a great picture," regardless of how anyone else looks. Or, you might say "let's retake that one" because you don't love the way you look. Just giving you a little something to think about here.

So now let's begin the deep dive into the principles that will prove to be priceless for your journey to be able to create, accomplish, give, and pass the one-month-off test!

Key Takeaways

- Apply the WHY-SMART framework to your personal, professional and financial goals.

- Expect a dip in your income when you are trying to grow your company. Make sure that you have enough money to cover you for three to six months as you train and ramp up your new employees.

- Pass the one-month-off test. If you fail, write down all of the areas where you failed and make sure to address them.

- Establish a morning routine.

- How much should you work?

- What will you do with your 24 hours each day?

- WHY-SMART goal setting model

- Understand and apply the 80/20 Principle.

- Law of Attraction

- Find your purpose.

- Be intentional.

- Practice humility.

- Treat everyone with respect and gratitude.

- Choose work you are passionate about.

- Always do the right thing.

- Continue to learn by reading books or engaging mentors.

Suggested Reading

- The Go-Giver by Bob Burg and John David Mann

- The 80/20 Principle by Richard Koch

Action Items

- Take the time to document your personal, professional, and financial goals using the WHY-SMART framework. Don't settle for easy goals. Stretch them a bit but limit your list to two or three goals. Come up with specific activities that you will do each day, each week and each month to move closer to your goals.

- Imagine that you cannot work for one month because of illness. Or that you need to be away to help a family member. Or you want to go on a well-deserved vacation for a month to pursue a lifelong dream. What areas of your business will get neglected as a result of your absence? Why? What will happen to your clients? To your employees? To your income? Come up with a list along with a solution to each one to prevent those problems.

- Calculate how much money you need per month to cover your expenses (house, car, food and other expenses). Start a savings plan to build a reserve that can last you at least six months. You'll need this money as a cushion as you grow your business.

- List 12 topics that you'd like to improve on or learn more about over the next year. What book do you need to read and/or what training do you need to take?

- Schedule now to be off for one month in a year from now. Put this on your calendar.

CHAPTER 2

FINANCE

"Beware of little expenses. A small leak will sink a great ship."
—Benjamin Franklin

"Money was never a big motivation for me, except as a way to keep score. The real excitement is playing the game."
—Donald Trump

"Rule No. 1: Never lose money. Rule No. 2: Never forget Rule No. 1."
—Warren Buffett

Jenna, I want you to follow these four sequential steps when it comes to finances. First, you need to define your personal financial objective. Based on that, you'll be able to break it down into a manageable number that can be translated into annual financial goals for your business. Second, you must discern the differences between GAAP and the concept of Profit First to ensure that your business will thrive. Third, we'll talk about automation and technology and how your choice of accounting software will influence how you run your business. Your choice of software will impact how you will create, track and manage your budget. Fourth, you must learn to manage your time and competing priorities. With a calendar, you'll be able to manage your schedule so that you will not be distracted and stressed out by unexpected personal or professional events that will come your way.

Goals

Jenna, as I gave some thought about how to organize this information for you, I went back and forth quite a bit about the best order. There are so many ways and so many different schools of thought about the cart and the horse. You may be too young to remember that one. Anyway, I'm making my best effort to give this information to you in an order that will make the most sense. So I will begin with finances.

First, I believe that every task we begin should start by considering what outcome we are hoping for. So, let's discuss your financial goals first. There's no right or wrong about a person's goals. Goals are personal and only you can decide what you want.

Here is something to think about... Try to figure out first, what your long-term objectives are, and then consider your short-term action steps. Let's say you want to retire at age 65 and you need to have a predetermined amount of money. Well, in order to accumulate that predetermined amount of money, you will need to begin saving now and incrementally contribute to it over time.

The other thing to consider for your business is how much money you will need for operating expenses each month. You need to develop a very specific budget and monitor that budget at least monthly. Most importantly, always, always live by the budget.

Before we look in greater detail about how to construct a budget and where to construct a budget, I want to talk about a fundamental principle that should determine how you budget.

GAAP vs Profit First Accounting

GAAP stands for Generally Accepted Accounting Principles. The GAAP would give you the logic that says your profit in a business is what is left over after your expenses. In other words, gross revenue less expenses equals profit. The problem too many business owners have, me included, is that their expenses too often do not include themselves. So, they end up just getting what's left over.

In his book, **Profit First**, Michalowicz tells about a fascinating and very unique principle where gross revenue, minus profit equals expenses. That may sound crazy to you at first, but think about it this way. Your business makes a specific amount of money in a given month. If you spend all the money that you owe for all the expenses due, you end up with too little money leftover to pay yourself. The risk is that you believe this is a situation for only this month and next month will be different. The problem all too often is that business owners experience this same situation every month until it becomes the norm. Without paying close attention, that experience will extend too many years. What Mike talks about in his book and what I believe completely, is that you should set aside a portion of your cash inflows as profit ... *first*. I began this practice many years ago and it has been very successful for me. It's called, "Profit First" accounting. I will emphasize the concept this way... Your business will make a specific amount of money each month and you will pay yourself a predetermined amount each month... no matter what. You may also claim a specific amount of profit and move that profit into a different checking or savings account, so that it's not commingled with your operating money. Then, what's left over is the money that is available to pay your expenses. Now you may say, "What if that's not enough money to pay the expenses that I owe?" That's a great question! Here's the answer. You will make it work! You will figure out very quickly how to get those bills paid. I've seen it happen many times. We tend to work harder to pay others than we do to pay ourselves. If you have a predetermined fair compensation for yourself, and fair profit margins; then, in my experience, a good business owner will figure out each month how to pay their expenses.

Let's say that your agency brings in $10,000 in gross revenue per month. You may want to set aside $4,000 of that as a salary for yourself and 10% ($1,000) as a profit for your business.

$10,000 gross revenue minus $4,000 for your salary minus $1,000 reasonable 10% profit = $5,000 left to pay your other business expenses like salaries of others and all operating costs.

While you may want to make more than $4,000 per month, it would be unreasonable to pay yourself more than that at the moment.

Now, let's say you hire three insurance sales agents with each bringing an additional $10,000 in monthly revenue for the agency. Now, the total will be $40,000 gross monthly revenue. Your ten percent profit is now $4,000 rather than $1,000 monthly. The three of them will get paid their usual salary and you, the business owner, will collect a profit of $4,000 for yourself in addition to your salary. If you were to hire ten agents, then you will be collecting the same 10% profit which will yield about $10,000 each month for you... in addition to your growing salary.

Remember that the 10% profit is just a starting point. As you grow, you'll gain the economies of scale, so your expenses per insurance sales agent will not necessarily stay at $5,000 each. If you are also working as one of the insurance sales agents, you'll bring in your own salary ($4,000 per month) plus the 10% profit that you'll collect from the business. At any point, if you decide not to be actively involved in the business, you'll always have the business profit to rely on.

WARNING: You cannot expect to work 100% as an insurance sales agent while growing your business. So, you need to set a manageable percentage of your time to keep generating income (example: 50% of your time) with the other half allocated to recruiting, training and coaching your sales team. As such, you should only collect 50% of your allocated salary ($2,000) plus the 10% profit that you set aside for the business. This dip in personal income is temporary and as your company grows, you should be able to receive a more reasonable salary and, hopefully, a higher profit margin. You also cannot expect your new agents to be operating at 100%. There is a bit of a learning curve, so it will take time before they are able to generate the same amount of revenue as you. Make sure that you are prepared financially; you personally and the business for this revenue fluctuation.

By the way, have you ever heard of Parkinson's Law? Parkinson's Law is the adage that "work expands so as to fill the time available for its completion." It is sometimes applied to the growth of bureaucracy in an organization. I have seen it work in other areas also; like for example, you buy a new home and one of the things you love about that new home is that you have tons more closet space than in your previous home. What always happens is that after you have been in the new home for a while, you realize that you have filled up your new closet just like you did your old one. Another common example is what can happen when you get a raise. You are excited to have this extra money available to add to your savings. Then, before you know it, you seem to be spending all of the "new" money just as before you had it. You realize that it doesn't even feel like you are making more than before. My point here is that if you pay yourself first, then are obligated to pay all the other expenses, you will find a way. If you do the reverse, you are more likely to short change yourself because much or all of the money you hoped to have left over to pay yourself will be gone.

Automation and technology

Jenna - now let's talk about a subject that is near and dear to my heart - technology. I've been a big believer for many years that in everything we do, we need to consider if it can be done more efficiently. I believe that started out as a personal challenge for me.

I have no idea why, but I viewed it as sort of a game to make things better, faster, more accurate and more efficient. After college, I became really interested in technology. That said, you are going to want to use accounting software that you enjoy. In physical fitness, I've heard that the best kind of exercise is the kind that you will do. I believe that's true here as well. You're going to want to use an accounting software program that you do not dread using. I have used QuickBooks for over 20 years. I love **QuickBooks**. I love the reporting, and I especially love the budgeting feature. I think a budget is incredibly important.

So, let's talk a minute about how to automate your budget. I recommend taking as much time as needed during November or December to build your budget for the following year. This might be one full day or multiple days. You need to be relaxed and possibly offsite if that helps you think better. You need to take your time in creating next year's budget. This is kind of fun for me. You start at the top of income, either alphabetically or sorting by your biggest expense items. I like sorting with my biggest expenses at the top. Look at your previous year's numbers. From there, you begin building your monthly income for each line item and then your monthly expenses for each line item. If you don't like numbers, this may not be fun for you. I think this is a blast! It's critical to know in order to effectively run your business. First of all, pulling out your income month by month, you should always expect to grow. You should budget for an increase each month. Whether that's 1% growth per month or 10% growth per month over the previous month, at least plan for growth. Using WHY-SMART goals, make sure that your growth plans are realistic. Do not budget for flat income. In the years that I budgeted for flat, that's what I got. In the years I budgeted for growth, that's what I got. What happens when you budget for growth? That becomes your goal and you figure out the action steps needed to reach that goal.

Be transparent

Being transparent with your finances is not easy. I have been transparent with my finances just as many successful companies are. Meaning, I have shared our income information with our entire Jenesis team for many years. The first fifteen years I was in business, I was not comfortable sharing our income. For some reason, I felt like that was private and none of anyone's business, even those who worked in my business. Wow! None of their business. That sounds so bad now when I hear myself say it. Anyway, after a lot of reading and after attending a lot of conferences over the years, I learned that when you work with the right people, there is no need to hide finances. Some people don't want to share finances because they don't want their employees to know how much money the business has generated. Again, that sounds so funny when I hear myself say it out loud. Let me say it again. Many businesses *do not want those who are an integral part of building that business to know how much money is coming into the business.* Such an odd thought process now that I think about it.

Anyway, about 15 years after I had been in business, I got better at having consistent team meetings (we'll talk about that later). I also got better at hiring the right people, treating those people better, and partnering with them in every way. So at each meeting, we started sharing the company income for the past month and the past quarter and the past year.

We also looked at where the money was coming from. That became a huge deal. When we were transparent about where the money was coming from, it made people think differently about what we all needed to do to increase income in the right places. The other thing that's interesting is... I believe when we are not transparent with our income, people tend to believe it's even more than it really is. So, if we're worried that the people on our team are going to see how much money is coming in and will greedily want a bigger part of that, we have more than one problem on our hands. One problem could be that team members believe we're not paying enough. Another could be that we're not working with the right people. My dad used to have a phrase that he said from time to time. He would say, "Eddie, I suggest you do *this* rather than that. I know which one is best because I have tried it both ways." He was a wise businessman. So, I will tell you Jenna, I have tried it both ways. Transparency is the way to go.

Use credit cards, but be smart - Pay off the balance monthly

Credit cards are a delicate subject for me. In my lifetime, I have been smart for the most part with credit card use. There were a few times in my thirties when I spent too much money on credit cards, and it took several months to pay off the balance. Never let that happen. Never let that happen. Never let that happen! (That wasn't a typo.) By the way, it's important that you never let that happen. Credit cards can be a great tool when used correctly. The correct way to use a credit card, in my opinion, is to make sure you are getting points or cash back in some way. Put as many things on the card for your business as you can, but those things need to be expenses that you would have had (even if you were not using a card). Then, pay the credit card off completely by the due date every month without fail. Never let the fact that you have a card allow you to make a decision to purchase something that you don't need or cannot afford. If you have a bad experience with a credit card, identify that early on and stop using the credit card. The value of a credit card is not great enough to jeopardize your financial well-being.

Keep debt low

When I started my insurance agency in 1991, I borrowed $4,000 from a local bank. I used that $4,000 to buy one filing cabinet that was around $100. I bought a computer that was a little more than $1,000. I brought a desk I had at home to the office. I rented an office for $125 a month, so it needed a little work. I bought carpet and had a friend of mine install the carpet and I painted the walls. With less than a $4,000 investment, I was in business. I had lettering put on the window which was pretty inexpensive, but I did not have enough money to buy a sign. I was able to pay that $4,000 off within a year.

The next time I went in debt, if I remember correctly, was about six years later when I purchased a small agency in my town. I believe the agency was around $100,000, and I borrowed that money from my dad. I paid him a 8% interest for either 24 or 36 months. I was never a day late on a payment and that income generated from the acquisition more than made that payment for me. So again, I borrowed $100,000, but I paid it off in no longer than three years.

I purchased three other agencies over the next few years using the same model. On two of those purchases, the previous owner financed most of the acquisition cost and I paid them off in three years. In every case, the income from the acquisition, more than made the payment for me. After those few acquisitions in the early days, I never went in business debt again. I'm not saying there's not the right time for it if it's an amazing investment. What I am saying is that it's best to save money and have the cash, rather than borrow money to invest. When I sold Carolina Insurance in January of 2018, it was debt free. I'm blessed today that there is no debt at Jenesis Software.

Establishing an accounting calendar

One thing that helps us succeed in accomplishing goals and completing specific tasks related to business finance and accounting, is adding events and deadlines on our calendars. For many things, calendars are better than to-do lists. We often create a to-do list and each day, mark a few things off and add a few things. At the end of the day, we either keep that to-do list as a running list or we move the unfinished items to the next day's to-do list. The problem with this is that the list becomes stressful and never ends. So, as it relates to business finances, I've had the most luck by putting events on my calendar. These are things that are done daily, weekly, monthly, quarterly, and annually.

Here's what I'm talking about...

Daily

The finances are someone's job in your company and when you're starting out, that someone is you. For example, you have to pay the bills and deposit the money. I believe that is a daily activity. If that's on your calendar for every morning at 9 a.m. or every evening at 5 p.m. (or possibly both), then that's the time you block out so you don't get behind on those tasks. Also, because it's on your calendar, you will have a better picture of your workload and responsibilities.

Weekly

The kinds of things you might want to do weekly could be to have a short meeting with team members about finances in their particular area or to have a quick 15-minute weekly budget review. If a weekly calendar item about finances does not click with you, then don't do that now. Keep it simple.

Monthly

I believe that a monthly calendar event to review the previous month's income and expenses as it compares to budget is non-negotiable. Depending on the size of your business and your income, that weekly meeting by yourself or with key people on your team could range from thirty minutes to half of the day. This is where you will review your income and your expense line items for the previous month and how that compares to your budget. You examine and understand areas where you did not meet budget and areas where you outperformed the budget. This is also where you need to create a pause moment. For example, if there is an area where you spent more than you planned to spend or your income was less than you planned it to be, then I recommend taking a moment to look at your year-to-date numbers. Your year-to-date through last month may be fine and you learn that it was just that last month has a small hiccup. If, however, your year-to-date income is trailing behind budget or your expenses in any given area are more than you planned, then you must make adjustments today. The trick and the best practice is not to alter your budget, but rather alter your habits. If you have spent more on marketing than you budgeted, but you spent less on supplies, then maybe you are okay. The bottom line still works in the budget. This may be where you will want to consider adjusting specific budget line items up or down in future months to match the expected reality.

Quarterly

Just like weekly, quarterly activities can be up to you. If you see the value and enjoy monitoring finances quarterly, it could be a one or two-hour meeting just for you or with key people to review the actual vs budget number for the previous quarter.

Annually

The annual meeting for yourself and/or with key people on your team is a big one. This is where you will sit down sometime in December and review the entire year to date. I recommend doing this in December even though the year is not quite complete because it's almost a 100% accurate picture. Plus, it's often a great time, when your mind is a little more at rest because of the holiday season (or at least for me it works that way), and you're able to not only review this past year but also to create your new financial budget goals for the upcoming year. It's also the time to come up with the action steps that are required to meet those goals and to establish a budget that includes realistic growth and realistic expenses.

Key Takeaways

- Use this year's actual profit and loss statement as a foundation for next year's budget.

- Budget for growth in income. In the early years of your business, growth could easily be 30% to 50%, but after five to ten years, it may be challenging to maintain double-digit growth. Always forecast for no less than 10% growth.

- Budget smart by researching and using standard percentages as guidelines for income growth and expenses. For example, I like 10% for marketing expense because that's the statistic I have seen most in my research.

- How does the 80/20 principle apply to finances and budget? Know this and use it.

- Keep debt low.

- Outsource when it makes sense.

- Use credit cards, but be smart - Pay balance monthly.

- Be transparent with finances.

- Each month, review your bank account balance your income compared to the same month last year, your actual results versus what you budgeted, and if you have customers paying you directly, your past due accounts.

Suggested Reading

- Profit First by Mike Michalowicz

Action Steps

- Enter your recurring calendar dates now.

CHAPTER **3**

LEADERSHIP

"Leadership is about making others better as a result of your presence and making sure that the impact lasts in your absence."
—Sheryl Sanberg, COO of Facebook

"If your actions create a legacy that inspires others to dream more, learn more, do more and become more, then, you are an excellent leader."
—Dolly Parton, Actress and Singer

"Leaders are made, they are not born. They are made by hard effort, which is the price which all of us must pay to achieve any goal that is worthwhile."
—Vince Lombardi, American Football Coach, and NFL Executive

"You are the average of the five people you spend the most time with."
—Jim Rohn

"The first job of leadership is to love people. Leadership without love is manipulation."
—Rick Warren

When you hear of the word leadership, Jenna, what's the first thing that comes to your mind? To me, the most important thing about being an effective leader is communicating your mission and vision to the entire organization. This must be very clear to you and you must ensure that your team shares the same clarity. In addition to communicating your mission, three other key components constitute an effective leader: delegating, coaching and mentoring. So, we'll talk about these as well. The last two components, coaching and mentoring, are geared for self-improvement and enable you to continue to excel as a leader. As such, you must always continue to learn either by reading or through mentoring; and finding a business coach will accelerate your progress. Are you excited to learn about these four topics?

Leadership goals

By now you understand the WHY-SMART goal framework. So, you will apply that framework to your leadership objectives here.

Delegation, coaching, and mentoring

Everyone is a leader. Regardless of your role in a company or in a family, you have leadership responsibilities. Good leaders are always coaching, cultivating and building leaders out of everyone on the team.

It is very important to communicate your mission and vision. Everyone on the team should have the same clarity and understanding of the objectives. This requires that YOU have clear goals and objectives. You communicate these goals and objectives every day in many ways. The actions that you take each day speak volumes to your team about what's important to you. The written communication that circulates internally and externally from your company speaks volumes about what's important to you and the company. So be very careful not to confuse people with inconsistent messaging. Keep your values aligned. Stay focused on the action items that are needed to reach your objective. Be careful not to lose focus (which I have done so often), and let other activities take you off track.

One of the big parts of leading is helping. The term **leadership** and the word **leading** say it all. You're not pushing; you're not demanding. You are helping people and leading them on a journey. In order for this journey to be truly successful and fulfilling for you and everyone else, including your team and your customers, this journey needs to be fun and rewarding. It will not be all of these things all the time - that's just not realistic. But you will need to be always aware of the importance of happiness and satisfaction.

Before you provide a solution to a problem, ask for their ideas. An important note about leadership is one that I forget too often. It's very simple and it's very specific. One of the greatest tricks to leadership, and to building leaders, is remembering not to answer every question everyone has. Give them an opportunity to answer their own questions. What I mean by this is if someone comes to you and says, "Jenna, how do you want me to do this?" or "How should I handle this situation?" be careful not to let your mind quickly jump into "solution mode." First take a deep breath, smile, relax and ask them what they think we should do about the situation. Let them give you one or two options. Ask them what they would do if you were not available for the answer. They could possibly go to another team member to gather insight. They could possibly Google and research for an answer. After you let them go through this exercise for a few moments (try to make it fun and don't make it miserable or put them on the spot), be sure to compliment them on their thought process even if they did not come up with the best answer in your opinion. Pat them on the back for giving this so much thought! Once you decide on a solution, take a moment to discuss and make sure you get agreement from them and that they understand why that is a good solution. You may even want to go back over the options they came up with that were not good. Let them think through these and discuss with you why those may not have been the best solutions. We all need to understand **Why**. Simply memorizing the answer to something does not help us remember it and become better. Gaining an understanding as to WHY things are the way they are helps us retain information and therefore be able to apply our knowledge to future situations.

Delegating is much harder than one would expect and there are a few reasons why. I will discuss three of the most common. One reason is that you may believe you will or could do it better. Another reason is that you can or could do it faster than the time it takes to teach someone else. The third reason could be that you get satisfaction (and possibly recognition) from being the one who gets things done.

There are many problems with those reasons not to delegate. Let's start with the first reason which is quality of work. It may be true that you can do it better. The problem is that model will not scale. You can't do everything. You may have heard this saying, "those who can't do...teach." I strongly disagree with that statement. I believe that "Those who care...teach". I also believe that "Those who can't teach, do!" To be a leader is to be a teacher, mentor and/or coach, whatever you want to call it.

Now let's discuss the second reason you may not want to delegate, which is because you could do it faster. That may be true... this time. What about the next time? And the time after that, and on and on. By taking the time to teach people how to do things, you are investing in your future, the future of your company and most importantly, you are investing in their future. If you just take the time to teach them to do things well, then every time that task comes along, you'll have someone dependable and qualified to perform the task.

And finally, if your reason to not delegate is because of the satisfaction and recognition you get from being the one who can do so many things, that is also a short-lived victory. In order for you to pass the "one month off test," or hopefully someday, the "one year off test," you absolutely must build a team of leaders through delegation and coaching.

You have permission to go back

There will be times when you say to yourself, "I wish I had done this" or "I wish I had done that differently." Anytime you find yourself feeling that way, remember that you have permission to go back and redo whatever it was. For example, there have been times when I would have a meeting with a team member and after that meeting, think of something I wish I had said or done differently. In my early days, I would just kick myself for forgetting it or for not thinking of that great idea. Then, a business coach I worked with Harvey Smith, taught me the concept of... you have permission to go back. What this means is that when you realize you should've done something differently, call that person. Schedule another meeting if needed. Sit down with them again and be transparent by saying something like, "after our meeting, I thought more about that situation and here are some additional thoughts I would like to share with you." This doesn't have to be just about meetings. It can be about anything that you find yourself wishing you had done differently in life. There are some things that are difficult or maybe impossible to go back and redo, but consider all of those things carefully and make sure that there is no way to improve the outcome of the situation based on your new idea or thought process.

Always learn and improve - Leaders are made, not born

I can not think of one skill that we are born with. When we are born, we can't dress or feed ourselves. We can't talk. We can't read or walk. We are pretty much useless. You were super cute, but let's be honest...you were more trouble than help there for a while. But through thousands of hours of coaching and mentoring from those around you, you finally learned how to walk, talk, read, feed yourself, reason, laugh, understand humor and complex concepts... and the list goes on and on. Some people in history are now considered to be, "great leaders." However, they all made mistakes along the way and they all improved, as leaders with experience should. Each leader is unique, which means you will not be like any other leader... and that's awesome! You may not be a perfect Steve Jobs or Bill Gates, but you will be the perfect you. As a matter of fact, there is no one else in the world that can be as good at being you ... as you! Embrace your personality and style and gifts. Invest time into learning principles of great leaders, and apply those principles to your own unique way of thinking and doing things.

Who are your mentors?

To learn how to do anything, like learning how to become a better leader, can be done through trial and error or through a proactive intentional process to become better. Trial and error work, but it's slow, painful, and expensive. Being proactive is a much better method. And there are so many ways that we can get better at anything. I recommend that you have mentors - not just one mentor and not the same mentors for your entire career. Different mentors come in and out of your life over time. This helps you become better in all aspects of your life. It doesn't have to be just work-related, it can be personal as well. We need to be better at relationships, therefore we need to associate, spend time with, and ask questions of people who are successful at relationships. We need to model what they do and understand their habits. Similarly, if we want to improve our level of health and fitness, we need to associate with, watch, model ourselves after, and ask questions of people who have been successful at being healthy. If we want to improve our spiritual lives, we find those people who have been successful with it and let them mentor us as we improve. Having a mentor can be an official relationship like working with a business coach. It can also be less formal; such as, developing friendships and relationships with people that are partly social and partly business. Make an effort and set goals to always have at least one active mentor in your life. I'm not suggesting ten or twenty mentors, because that gets complicated. Always have one or two mentors in your life, and they can come in and out of your life based on your need.

Leaders are readers

Most successful leaders seem to read a lot. I read a lot now, but didn't in the early days. It's like everything else... if you make the effort, it will become easier and become a habit.

I don't mean read one or two books a year. I recommend more like one a month or even one a week. Some people say that they are just not readers and they don't really like to read. Well, you need to read Jenna. If sitting down for 15 to 30 minutes a day, every morning or every day at lunch or every evening, and reading a chapter of a book is miserable and you find yourself just not doing it; then, figure out what works for you. You could possibly even purchase the audiobook version. Maybe you could listen to 15 to 30 minutes of that or even one chapter each day. Maybe when you hear about a good book, or if someone recommends a book related to your subject matter, you could spend 15 to 30 minutes that day on YouTube watching book reviews that other people have done and explain what they got out of that book. Figure out what works for you. Then, begin to consume content that other people have created. That becomes a form of a mentor. Don't try to figure everything out by yourself. Read and learn what other people have learned who have gone before you. You don't have to agree with everything but, analyze it. If you disagree, decide why you disagree. I think the key to being successful with reading is to set realistic daily goals. I believe that rather than trying to find an hour or two hours in a day or week to read, it's best and most effective to create a habit of 15 to 30 minutes daily and do your best to stick to it.

Accelerate progress with a business coach

I began working with a business coach in 2012. I love this idea. Your business coach does not have to be smarter than you are or more successful. Your business coach needs to be someone who cares about you and your success. Your business coach needs to be someone who has relevant experience and who will be honest with you. Your business coach should be someone who will see you from a different perspective. He or she will identify more of your blind spots than you will be able to see. A business coach is not necessarily an accountability coach but, in my experience, that becomes a big part of what makes the relationship successful. If your business coach identifies something that was not as clear to you and helps establish a path for you to resolve that issue, then you're more likely to be successful accomplishing that task because you're accountable to someone.

Encourage and celebrate

This is another area that I did not get right early on. I'm not sure what influenced me back then, but for some reason, I felt like I was doing people a favor when I gave them a job. I felt like I was the boss and my job was to tell them what to do, how to do it, and when to do it. When they did what I asked, how I asked, and when I asked, I treated that as status quo. What I've learned over the years is that it's important to encourage and celebrate when people do things right. If we look at it as only celebrating the things that are above and beyond, we will have fewer opportunities to celebrate; mostly because the celebrations and encouragement are what enables a person to reach exceptional performance. So I encourage you (it's funny that I just said encourage you) to encourage others, compliment others, be interested in others, pay attention to others, and celebrate even the smallest of victories.

Kindness

How does kindness fit into business? I consider myself a technical person. Many technical people excuse their behavior and blame the way they act on the fact that they are technical. Interesting right? So if I am technical, I don't have to be nice? I think not. I have allowed myself over the years, and I'm ashamed to say still do from time to time, to not be kind because I may be busy. I doubt I do this with customers, but I definitely have done it with members of my team. Don't do that! Always be kind. If you are so stressed and so overwhelmed with your work that you are not kind and relaxed with your team, what kind of leader are you? Does lack of kindness make you look like you have things under control? Absolutely not. If you are so busy, stressed, and frustrated that you answer the phone when a team member calls and are anything less than kind and patient with them, you need to figure out how to fix that problem. When you have things under control, you are a good role model for your team.

Why?

When you ask someone to do something for you, it's very important you tell them why. There are two reasons for this. One reason is that when people understand why it helps them remember how. The second reason is that when people understand why; especially when they believe in the way; they are more likely to be diligent about the task and be thorough when accomplishing the task. I will throw in a bonus reason for this. When you ask someone to do something and you don't tell them why that really comes off as not being kind. It makes you sound bossy. But when you ask someone to do something and tell them why they're doing it; now you're including them in the entire project.

Help others be successful

Your entire job as a leader should be to help other people be successful. Every day you should be focused on serving the members of your team. Your job as a leader should include fewer to-do items, and more time spent with the team helping them. If you focus on helping your entire team be successful at what they do, then you've got this entire team of successful people. What do you think your business will look like if everyone on the team is successful? That's right. If everyone on your team is successful, your organization will be successful.

Redundancy in people: two can play at this game

Being a student of technology, I am a big believer in redundancy. Every effort needs to be made to never have a single point of failure. If this is true with technology, then it's also true with your team. If there is anyone in your organization, including yourself, who is the only person who can do a specific task well, then you need to be working on a plan to resolve that problem. We will talk more about this when we discuss human resources and your team.

Admit when you are wrong: "I was wroooo, I was wroooonnn"
Looking back over the years, I remember one time in 2002 when I was wrong. Just kidding! In 2002 I was probably wrong 2002 times! Every year, I am often wrong. The television sitcom "Happy Days" was before your time but one of the characters, Arthur Herbert Fonzarelli, aka Fonzie, or just, "The Fonz", was a super cool dude...much like me! (Sorry, I got carried away.) Anyway, when The Fonz was wrong, he would try to say he was wrong but all that came out was, "I was wrrrrr, I was wrooooo, I was wrooonnn". Then someone would normally just say, "It's ok Fonz". He, like many of us, has a very difficult time saying we are wrong. (You should YouTube "fonz wrong").

You will be wrong from time to time. The best courses of action after you realize you are wrong about something is to say, "I was wrong about that", and then figure out what your next step is. Never make an excuse for why you were wrong. Never waste time trying to explain your thought process and why you could have been right if only some things had gone differently. That's a waste of everyone's time. When you are wrong, say you are wrong, then move on. It sends a terrible message to your team when you correct them when they are wrong, and then, be in denial when you are.

Spaced repetition

Again, I have to give credit to a business coach I worked with, Harvey Smith. When I started working with Harvey, one of my problems that I wanted him to help me solve was that many of my team members seem to continue to do things wrong even after I had told them how to do it! I was frustrated and my frustration came across to others. There may be a few people out there that you were able to tell one time how to do many things and they do it right from then on. I think those people are very rare. I believe that the way to get people to consistently do things the way you want them to do it is to first explain the process well. Then explain the "why." Make sure you have agreement from people, which they understand, and will do what you ask. After all of that, the next step is to use spaced repetition as needed to help them stay on track. You may be thinking, well that's a bummer, I wish I could just tell people one time and then they would do it right forever! Well, you have two options. One option is to keep on hoping that. (And probably be disappointed many times.) Your second option is to explain things well, tell them why, get an agreement that they understand and plan to do this thing you've asked, and then remind them from time to time when and how to do the thing you've asked.

Let me add, I don't mean it's acceptable to ask someone to come to work at 8:45, then for them to continually be late, and for you to remind them every day. If you tell someone to come in at 8:45 and they do pretty well for a week or two and then they miss a couple of days, you may want to remind them. Explain to them why you think it is important that they are there on time, and ask them if we can agree that they are going to be there at that time going forward. Then, if they do pretty well for a couple of months and are then late a couple of days, you may need to have that conversation again. This process should enable them to do things well most of the time, and over time, should increase their effectiveness. This is not an excuse for people to perform poorly often. You must sometimes make the decision that enough is enough and it's time to part ways.

Lead by example

Words are cheap. Actions speak louder than words. People watch you when you don't know they are watching. Don't tell someone to do something that you are not able or willing to do yourself. I am not talking about not asking your accountant to do your taxes unless you have the same qualifications. I don't expect you to know how to do everything or be qualified to perform every task. However, I do recommend you "walk the walk" in terms of core principles you teach and ask of your team, such things as integrity and work ethic, for example. If you say your organization is "transparent," always be "transparent."

Say "thank you" often and sincerely

This is so easy, yet so many leaders simply forget to say, "thank you." If you feel like saying thank you too much diminishes its value, then think again. A leadership course I took a few years ago advocated saying thank you to your team three times as much as you think you should. When someone calls you to say they finished their part of that project, don't go right into asking questions like, "how long did it take?" or "did you have any problems?" Start by saying, "thank you for doing that." Then, ask your questions. Then, finish by saying thank you again. When someone sends you an email to say they called that customer back and resolved their issue say, "Wow, thanks so much for doing that. You handled that quickly and I really appreciate it." To keep your thank yous from getting too routine, change up how you say thank you. Change the phrase around and add to it, so it's not just a simple "thanks" every time. Thank them face to face, via email, over the phone, publicly in front of customers and other team members. Also, remember that showing gratitude and saying thank you is not a one-way street. It's not just what a leader should do towards the team that reports to them. It should also be how team members treat each other. How you treat your boss. How you treat your customers. How you treat those who provide a service to you when you are their customer. How you treat your family and friends. One last thing. Don't keep score. Simply show gratitude and don't think twice about how others are showing their gratitude. You are in charge of you and they are in charge of themselves. Remember when I said you should lead by example? This is one way you can do that.

Key Takeaways

- Create leadership goals.

- Delegate.

- Coach and mentor others.

- Before you provide a solution to a problem, ask for their ideas.

- You have permission to go back!

- Always be learning and improving.

- Leaders are made, not born.

- Use mentors.

- Leaders are readers.

- Work with a business coach.

- Encourage others.

- Celebrate the successes of others. Both small and large victories.

- Be kind to everyone, all the time!

- Always explain the **WHY**.

- Help others be successful.

- Redundancy in people

- Admit quickly and sincerely when you are wrong or make a mistake.

- Use spaced repetition.

- Lead by example.

- Say thank you often and sincerely. Show appreciation.

Suggested Reading

- How to Win Friends and Influence People by Dale Carnegie

- Leadership 101 by John Maxwell

- The One Minute Manager by Ken Blanchard

- CEO Flow by Aaron Ross

Action Steps

- Add research time, then schedule an interview with a few business coaches.

- Add research time, then request a meeting with a few possible mentors.

- Schedule a daily reading time.

- Create one WHY-SMART goal for leadership.

CHAPTER **4**

MARKETING

"The cost of being wrong is less than the cost of doing nothing."
—Seth Godin

What is marketing?

Marketing and Sales are often considered the same thing. However, marketing is the process of promoting your product or service and generating leads. Sales take over after the marketing process has brought a prospect to the table.

First, establish a marketing budget

No return without an investment

The fundamental concept to understand in business and in life is that every desired outcome requires an investment. If you would like to be physically fit, you have to invest in nutrition and exercise. If you want to be loved, you have to first love. If you want to have more wealth, you have to invest labor or money.

If you would like to get more customers than you currently have, an investment is required. I say all of this because I often see, and have been guilty of this myself, people try to grow their business without having any idea or plan as to how much money they're going to invest, why they're investing, and exactly what they're going to invest this money in.

The question is, should you start by figuring out where you need to invest your money for marketing and then how much that will cost, or should you determine how much you're going to spend, and then decide where you are going to spend it?

The old saying about the cart and the horse applies here. Which do you decide first: where you need to spend your money, or how much money to spend?

I think about that as I analyze this concept of marketing decisions coming before the budget or the budget coming before the marketing plan. Do you create a budget then decide how to spend that money or do you decide what marketing is going to cost for what you want to do and then set the budget to support that?

I believe that your budget coming first. We've already discussed the budget, and we've already mentioned that budgets are based on the previous year's experience, what you plan and hope for an outcome, and the industry standards that you've researched.

When you research marketing, you can find some companies are spending as little as zero money on marketing and others are spending as much as 75% of their gross income on marketing. I believe if your past experience tells you that you can spend zero money on marketing and grow as fast as you would like to grow, then that is exactly what you should do. If you do not have a history yet to pull from, or if you would like the future to be different than the past has been, I suggest investing more money than you have in previous years or using a standard rule-of-thumb percentage like 10%.

Monitor and measure results

Track marketing expenses carefully in your accounting system. In QuickBooks, I create a category called marketing and subcategories like Direct Mail, Social Media, Website, etc. You should review monthly, quarterly, and annually to make sure your spending is getting the desired result in each area.

Know the lifetime value of your average customer. If you don't know how much a customer is worth, it will be difficult to know how much you can spend to acquire a customer. We will talk more about this when we talk about sales.

Establish the marketing plan

What's been the source of your customers so far?

Once we have determined how much money we can spend, then we can create a plan for how we're going to spend that money. There are essentially two ways we can start thinking about how we're going to choose what to spend your money on. One way is to look at our history of where we have been getting customers. Most of my career in my agency we have used our agency management system, Jenesis, to accomplish this. Using Jenesis, we were always diligent about tracking the source of every policy that we wrote. Then, we could run reports and know if a customer who purchased a homeowners insurance policy last month found us from our website, was a referral to our agency, or had other types of insurance with us already. I really enjoy looking at these reports from the previous year, grouping them, and sorting them by the most success. I love seeing referrals at the top because the closing ratio for referrals is higher as is the retention of customers who have been referred to you. You see this in reports that you run in your agency management system. I then like to consider each of those areas like referrals, other advertising efforts, and ask myself for each one, 1) How much money are we spending to create that now, and 2) What could we do to increase that? For example, let's say your number one source is referrals. It's likely you are spending very little money to create referrals, which is part of the beauty. But, it's important to read and study ways that other businesses and insurance agencies are increasing referrals. For example, you can have a referral program where each person who sends you a referral is entered into a drawing to win something or is given an gift card to a local business for each referral. This does two things. People like gifts and they will refer more new customers to you. It also supports local business, which in turn may allow you to write insurance for those businesses and possibly for their employees. If you do this, then it is marketing money you are spending to try to increase referrals.

What's not working for you?

The second place to look after you consider what has worked in the past and how do we increase that are the areas where you're not getting business from today. As you read, research, and work with mentors, you will always come across new and innovative possibilities that you may want to try. Consider these carefully, and test with enough investment to at least give it a good try, but be conservative and not gamble unwisely. These could be things like purchasing leads. If you have not purchased leads in the past, and you do not have a track record of success or failure, research what others are doing and what's working and then budget a specific, affordable amount to test this for long enough to know if it's working or not. For example, a 30-day test would not be realistic, a year may not be required, but in my opinion, at least six months is needed to truly understand if this is going to be something that may work or not.

We talked a lot about goals. We talked about the importance of them being written. It is also helpful with your marketing plan to create a written plan. Put this somewhere that works for you. It could be a MS Word document on your computer, it could be on Yammer or Slack, or it could be in Google Docs. Put it where you enjoy working and where you will be able to create a safe home for it, so you're able to keep the original copy.

In your marketing document, begin by listing everything that comes to your mind as methods for marketing. That list may start out looking something like this.

- Marketing Options
  - Website
    - Performance
    - Visitors
    - Conversions
  - Referrals
  - Email Marketing
  - Partnerships
  - Write a book
  - Social Media
    - Facebook
    - LinkedIn

After you have your draft of possible marketing methods, move the ones to the top that you feel would be the most effective. Then, under each one of these items begin writing in more detail what the plan could possibly be to utilize this method. Include with these notes estimated expense amounts. One of the big problems with marketing is people tend to be very inconsistent. There are so many things to choose from that many of us become overwhelmed and we'll do a little bit of something for a little while, then move to something else. Then, hear about a new thing and try that, and on and on and on. It's better to sort these with the ones at the top that you feel may be the most effective, describe what your plan is for that particular idea, and document your execution strategy. If you're building this plan at the end of the year for the coming year, consider creating a marketing calendar. In your marketing calendar, you can have deadlines for the different strategies you plan to implement, and it also acts as a good reminder to look back on and see when you took action on specific tactics.

Once you've gone through your list, established the items you are going to take action on, and spent your budget, leave the other items as possible future ideas. As you begin to implement the strategies, whether through internal implementation or outsourcing some of these things, be sure to add to your calendar monthly review times, so you analyze and measure the success of each one of them. As we said before, in order to measure the success, you will need to have established an objective for each one. It's important to establish this in the beginning. If you spend X amount of money per month for a result, then in six months you know what that result should look like. If the result is less than your established objective, it may be time to pull the plug on that particular marketing effort or at least a good time to review and make changes to that approach.

Outsourcing

Another thing I want to mention is outsourcing. Outsource everything you can. It's likely that you are not an expert in everything. That's a pretty safe bet. I know I sure have not been, even though I've tried often. There are some things that are so easy to outsource like accounting and marketing. If you love doing something, of course, you can consider keeping that in-house, but be careful that you don't keep too many of the wrong things for yourself just because you enjoy them. This all needs to come down to being happy and enjoying what you do, but sometimes we make decisions believing that this is what makes us happy and it might in the short-term, but may not in the long-term. If you are able to hire someone or a firm for your accounting and marketing, those people probably know what they are doing better than you will ever be able to do it. The big thing this does is let you focus on the other parts of the business that is much harder to outsource, like leadership.

Write a book

Over the years I have often thought about writing a book. I would have an idea that would come to my mind and I would think to myself, self, you should write a book one day. Then, I would forget about it for a while. A few years later, I would think about it again. Sometimes, because I heard about someone who had written a book and I thought that was kind of cool and I should do that too. Then, I would forget about it for a few more years. Anyway, I believe if most people could wave a magic wand and instantly be the author of a book, they would do it. I believe most people don't know where to start, what exactly to write about, and how it all works. I believe you should write a book. You should write a book because it is a great way to gain clarity around what's important to you. It's also a great way to map something out that you can use in your own life while at the same time sharing with others and hopefully helping others. Now, how does this fit in with marketing? If I'm the owner of an insurance agency or a software company, for example, and write a book that is relevant to the business I'm in, what a great way to position me and my company as someone who knows what they're talking about. So for example, the owner of an insurance agency could write a book about how to understand insurance, how to save money on insurance, how to find the right insurance agency, or how to run a business, and make that book available to their customers as a resource to help them be more successful. The book doesn't have to be long or amazing, publishing a book that's not great is still better than not publishing a book at all.

Website

My intention here is to give you information that will help you be successful in running a business, not to explain every nuance of every marketing strategy that exists. With that said, however, I do want to mention a couple of things about websites. You need to decide why you have a website. What is your goal? What do you want visitors to do when they go to your website? Most insurance agencies, just like us here at Jenesis, have a website that they hope will be instrumental in bringing them new customers, as well as help existing customers, find the information they need. On our Carolina Insurance website, it was important to track how many visitors came to the site each month. We wanted that number to grow, and we wanted to have action steps that we could work on that would influence how many people would visit our website. The second metric we wanted to look at was of the people who are visiting our website each month, how many were requesting information from us. For the most part, what we wanted to happen was for them to fill out a form to request a quote or give us a call. It's important to track every call in your agency management system accurately because it's possible people are calling your agency from your website and you're not really giving a website credit for being instrumental in the customer getting to you. If they fill out a form on the website to request a quote, then it's obvious they came from the website. But if they call, unless you are using call tracking, which I recommend, or being thorough about asking how that customer found you and enter that information in your agency management system, you may not know. So again, you should track the percentage of people who requested quotes because they visited the site and you should set goals to increase that number. Your action steps there would be things like making your website look different or having a different message. You should try different things to increase the number of visitors to your site and then the number of people who take action. These are normally called conversions and are the two most important things to measure your website's performance.

Don't stop doing what's working

A mistake I have made over and over and have seen others make is to stop doing things that work. I know this sounds absurd but if an activity is not on autopilot, it's so easy to get busy with other things and stop doing what's working. My advice here is to put everything you can on autopilot, and for those things that can not be automated, delegate and schedule meetings to review their progress. The meetings will be a time to review your checklist of marketing initiatives and to verify that each initiative is on track.

Marketing meetings

I do not promote meeting for the sake of meeting, but I have found that meetings can be a great way to stay focused. I recommend having a one-hour monthly marketing meeting. If you schedule recurring meetings for things like your marketing and include others in the meeting, it's a great way to hold one another accountable. During these meetings, you will want to have a checklist of things to review, such as your source report for the past month, quarter, or year.

Source

I want to know the top five sources of new customers during a time period. I want to know how it has changed from previous time periods. I also want to think about what can change to improve any sources we want to get more business from. For example, if the number of customers we got last month from the internet has increased, I will be happy. If the number has decreased, I will want to look deeper. Did the number of visitors to our site decrease? If that's true, then why? If the number of visitors did not decrease but the number of conversions and/or the number of people who requested a quote decreased, then I want to know why. Did our site change? If the same number or more people visit our site, but fewer have converted, something is wrong on the site and it's not an SEO (Search Engine Optimization) issue.

Know the lifetime value of a customer

We have a report in Jenesis for so many cool things to help with marketing. In addition to several source reports, we also have a lifetime value of a customer report. We need to know the lifetime value of an average customer before we can determine how much money we can invest to acquire a customer through our marketing.

For example, if the average insured stays with your agency for five years, pays $1,000 annually in total premium for one or more policies, and you average 12% commission, then your agency is going to make $600. You can do the math to see if your average customer stays with you less or more than five years and if the average annual premium is more or less than my example. The point here is that if you decide to purchase leads, pay $10 per lead, get ten leads per month, and close one of those, you are trading $100 for $1,000, which I would do all day long. Now, keep in mind that you do have costs associated with each customer, so you will not be able to pay the entire lifetime value of a customer just to get them. You will need to decide what your formula needs to be based on your expenses to bring on and service a customer. I would not want to pay more than 50% of the lifetime value to acquire a customer, but would expect to invest more than 10%.

Put marketing on autopilot

Use automation, delegation, and outsourcing to put marketing on autopilot. Anything that can be automated should be. Things that can normally be automated are things like email marketing from the agency management system for things like welcoming new customers, asking for referrals and referral thank yous to encourage more referrals. Things to delegate will be those things you are not able to automate, but have someone on staff that can do them like calling people back who called for a quote last year and did not buy. Things to outsource may be the design and maintenance of your website and SEO.

Enjoy the process

As with all aspects of your role in any business, I believe you should have fun. You should get satisfaction from the process. If you find yourself dreading any aspect of any process, and you will from time to time, stop and give thought to why. Discuss this feeling with your business coach and mentors. There will be a way for you to enjoy the process and it's up to you to find it.

Key Takeaways

- Establish the marketing budget.

- No return without an investment

- Establish the marketing plan.

- Source of current customers

- New possible sources of customers

- Outsource.

- Write a book.

- Keep your website up-to-date.

- Don't stop doing what's working.

- Schedule a monthly marketing meeting.

- Review source.

- Know the lifetime value of a customer.

- Put marketing on autopilot.

- Enjoy the process.

Suggested Reading

- Predictable Revenue by Aaron Ross

- Book Yourself Solid by Michael Port

Action Steps

- Enter your recurring monthly marketing review day on your calendar.

CHAPTER **5**

SALES

"What we dwell on is who we become."
—Oprah Winfrey

Jenna, selling your product or service is a critical part of being successful in business. So just like the other critical areas of business we have already discussed, setting goals is where it all starts. You will see it's true when we talk about customer service, and building and leading an exceptional team later. You must first decide what you want, then how to get it.

Many insurance agency owners started out as insurance agents working for an agency. That's exactly how I started. When they decided to open their own agency and become an entrepreneur, they think it will be easy because they are such good insurance agents. They know insurance backward and forwards so they assume it will be easy to be a successful agency owner. The problem is that there are other moving parts to running a business like leadership, marketing, sales, customer service, and human resources. It's rare that any one person is great at all of these parts. My point here is that you need to decide what you are great at and identify what you love, which will normally be the same thing, and you need to focus on doing those things well. You should outsource or delegate all tasks that you don't love or are not great at doing.

We hired you away from your teaching career to work in our agency, Carolina Insurance; you were an instant superstar in the areas of customer service, sales and pretty good at marketing. You had little opportunity to be tested in HR or leadership at that point. When we moved you from the agency to Jenesis, you instantly took to sales like a fish to water. So, sales will be an area you will want to stay close to throughout your career and possibly delegate other things like HR and marketing for example. When you delegate, as a leader, you will still be involved, but it will not be your daily focus. Also, just because you are talented in sales doesn't mean you do all the selling. It just means that if you love it and are great at it like you are, you should spend more time in that area of your business even if it's in a coaching capacity for other salespeople on your team.

Define sales goals

Let's start off by talking about goals again. Like I said before, it doesn't make any sense to establish a plan without having goals. How in the world would we know how to create a map if we have no idea of where we want to go?

So let's decide how much you want to grow this year. This can be based in part on what your sales were last year and in part on the budget that we've created. Now work backward to decide what your sales will need to be. When we know what our sales need to be this year, we can then break that down into monthly goals. Now we know what our monthly sales objectives are, which becomes a goal, is measurable, and we can then create the actions steps needed to achieve. Each of these actions steps can be sort of like a mini goal. They can each be measured and have time frames attached.

When setting your goals, decide specifically what you want to measure. Do you want to set your goal to have a specific number of active policies at a specific time? Do you want to have your goal focused more on premiums or more on gross revenue coming into your agency? Do you want to have more home policies, auto, or motorcycle? You may want a combination of these things and that's great. The important thing is to decide how many policies, and/or customers, and/or how much premium, and/or what your gross revenue will look like at a predetermined time and then create your action steps to achieve that.

I would again create a document much like the marketing plan, where you list your goals and action steps. Documentation can include your marketing because that's part of what's required in order to reach your sales goals. But your documentation is especially going to focus on the non-marketing activities you and/or your team have set that will result in you and your team reaching your objectives.

A good exercise might be to start by quickly listing all the activities that an agent can engage in that will result in increased sales. That list may look something like this.

- How to close a sell
- How to improve closing ratio
- How to cross-sell
- How to round accounts
- How to prospect
- How customer service is a sales function
- How to get more referrals

Once you have created a list of ways to improve sales, then go back through the list and move the ones to the top that you believe will get you the best results with the least effort. Remember the 80/20 rule; 20% of our efforts will result in 80% of our successes.

Once you have the top few areas that you want to focus on, document more information about each one.

Closing ratio

For example, if you want to improve closing ratio, you have to start by making sure you are measuring your closing ratio. In our software, we have always been diligent about tracking the quotes by each agent, and which ones have sold. We're able to calculate a closing ratio and set a goal for improving the ratio in the future. Make a list of action items under that goal that will be implemented to achieve the goal. That list may look something like this:

- Compare the closing ratios of all agents in the office and let those with higher ratios teach others.
- Research how to improve the closing ratio.
- Assign team members the task of researching how to improve.
- Make sure they are quoting all available companies.

When you have created a list of ways to improve closing ratio, for example, one of the ideas I mentioned above is assigning team members the task of researching specific areas, this can be very powerful. After the research has been done, agents can document their findings into a blog and post the blog on your site to share with customers to help them.

Although referrals may be something we work on in our marketing plan, sales and customer service is where we do the work that helps us succeed. So, it's critical to treat everyone with kindness and always do what's best for the customer. If you do that and provide a memorable experience, they will want others to benefit from your products and services.

Track and improve closing ratio

When I started my agency, we didn't have a great way to track our closing ratio. That was ok at first because it was just me for the first year anyway. Less than a decade later, I had created Jenesis, and part of what it did was track every quote and which ones were sold. Presto, we had our closing ratio.

Why is the closing ratio so important?
Think about this. Let's say you have two agents quoting in your agency. Each of them quotes a few policies each day. So, they may each quote say around 20 policies a week or 80 per month or 1,000 for the year.

Now let's imagine one of the agents normally closes 40% of their quotes and the other one closes 60%. At the end of the year, the one closing 40% will write 400 policies and the other agent will write 600 policies.

Let's calculate one more value. How much is a policy worth? What's the lifetime value of a policy? Let's say your average premium is $1,000 per year and you get paid 10% commission on average. I hope these are low numbers but they are easy to work with. Now, how long do you keep the average policy? Your system should give you this data. Let's say you keep the average policy for five years. Our commission on the average policy is $100 per year and we keep the average policy for five years, so the lifetime value of a policy is $500.

Let's go back to our two agents. The agent that closes 40% of what they quote will write 500 policies and generate $200,000 in commission for your agency. The agent who closes 60% of their quotes will write 600 policies and generate $300,000 in commission for your agency.

That's $100,000 in additional income generated by one person without spending any more money on marketing.

Account rounding and cross-selling

Account rounding to me is selling new coverages to an existing client like adding jewelry coverage to a home policy. Cross-selling is selling a new line of business to an existing client like selling a motorcycle or boat policy to a customer with a home or auto policy.

Right up there with referrals, great use of sales efforts is to have more of your existing clients buy more of your products and spend more money for each of them as a result of having better coverage. The more lines of business a customer has with you increases the time that customer will stay with you, which in turn increases the lifetime value of that customer. It should also be easier to sell other lines of business to an existing customer because you already have a relationship with them. It's also nice that it costs less to round and cross-sell than to acquire a new customer. Please don't misunderstand and think I am suggesting you sell someone something they don't need. I am just suggesting you make sure every customer has everything they need and that they are getting all they can from your agency.

If this is to be a goal, you have to start by measuring what you have now. You must then help your sales team set their goals to increase cross-selling and account rounding.

To incentivize or not to incentivize

Over the years I have gone back and forth with this one. I have seen very successful agencies that haveincentivized based on specific performance and I have also seen very successful agencies who did not pay any incentives at all.

We will discuss compensation more when we discuss HR and your team, but for now, let's think for just a moment about incentives as they apply to a sales team or salesperson.

This is going to be something you will need to decide how and if you want to do it. One thing to be aware of is that if you have started an incentive plan and do not feel it has changed behavior or increased performance, then it can sometimes be difficult to take the incentive away without adversely affecting morale. However, if a change is the right thing for the long term, then you need to pull off the bandage quickly and deal with a little short term pain.

We are all different and some people are motivated by money, some by praise and recognition, some by reaching a goal, and some by other factors. At the end of the day, the one constant in your business is you. So, it's important for you to build a team of people that you enjoy working with. Your team could be primarily motivated by money or primarily motivated by having a good time and being successful as part of a team working on common objectives. You get to choose who you work with.

I will leave you with this. In my experience, I have not enjoyed paying incentives or commission for performance where each person ends up being compensated differently. I have enjoyed compensating everyone with a salary, which is based on experience and contribution, fully paid company benefits, and a percentage each month of the growth of income compared to last year. Everyone on the team gets the same bonus each month and we are transparent about our growth or lack of.

Implement an ongoing training plan

Training can be a difficult goal to accomplish. There are a few reasons that it's difficult. Sometimes people do not feel like they need to be better than they are. Sometimes we are so busy with our day to day that it seems like a waste to take time away from doing what we're doing for more training. You need to read the" 7 Habits of Highly Effective People," and specifically, the chapter on sharpening the saw for an interesting perspective on this concept. Another reason could be that we don't want to spend the money on training. Another reason could be we are such a small business that we can't afford for people to be away from the office for training.

So why should people train? Are we as good as we need to be at everything we do? Can we be better? Should we be better? Is our competition getting better?

We can be lazy, so the easy thing to do is to come to work every day, do what we know how to do, and go home every evening. The problem is that this leads to burnout and boredom. When we learn, grow, and use our new knowledge to effect change in our business, it's exhilarating and exciting.

Once we decide that we need to get better at what we do, the question is what, how and when. I suggest making this one of your goals and creating action steps to research those very questions. If you're not currently doing any training, set a goal for this year to participate in one training program. This needs to be for each person in your organization. If you are a member of an association, check with them to see what education programs they have to help you in the area that you need help. Do you want to learn more about how a homeowners policy works, or do you want to learn more about how to be happy, successful, sell more, and communicate with your team better? You may also want to check online to see what kind of programs are available if you do not have time to go take a course somewhere.

Faced with a dilemma, I once heard a story about a manager who pondered the question: "If I train them, they may leave to get a better job. But what if I don't train them and they stay?"

Meet with the sales team

I suggest you have a weekly sales team meeting where you discuss the past week and the upcoming week. This meeting needs to be no longer than one hour. I also suggest you have a similar meeting monthly that needs to last no less than one hour. Finally, schedule quarterly sales team meetings that last no less than half a day. Do these quarterly meetings off-site if possible in a setting that stimulates happiness and creativity.

Part of all these meetings needs to be to review sales numbers and closing ratios. This information needs to always be at the forefront for everyone. We will discuss quarterly individual meetings when we discuss human resources and teams, but for now, I will just mention that a big part of your job is to help each salesperson create their goals.

Treat everyone with kindness

I know we have already talked about the importance of treating everyone with kindness, but I think it is worth repeating here as it relates to sales. I think that treating others well is reward enough because it's just the right thing to do. But, if that wasn't enough, there is more. Everyone you meet, even if you don't think it's possible, could be a source of new business. They could possibly buy insurance from you now or later, or they could refer you to someone who could buy. If you are on vacation and you encounter someone outside of what you think is your sales territory, you still need to take the time to treat them with respect. What if that person you meet while on vacation in another state knows someone who works with a carrier that you currently do not represent and would like to represent in your agency?

Close deals over the phone

When I first started my agency, before you were born, almost all new business was written in the office. Now, much, if not most, of new business is written over the phone or even through chat or email. All I want to mention here is to be aware of whatever makes it easier for your customer to do business with you and provide them with that experience. I have seen many agencies who still tell the prospect what the price of the insurance will be and when the prospect says, ok thanks, they both hang up the phone. Wow! I hope you learned better than that from me during the summers you worked in our agency when you were in college, and that it was reinforced when you left teaching to work at Carolina Insurance. During the phone call, when you are talking with the prospect to collect information to give them a quote, you want to be kind, use their name a couple of times, show interest in whatever they are insuring, and after you give them the rate, ask how that sounds. Regardless of how they answer, you have an opportunity to offer to process this for them right now over the phone, saving them a lot of time. If you do this every time, you will close more deals than if you don't, and you will do it then instead of later.

Common objections

One of the most common objections you will hear is the price. The problem with only winning when you have the least expensive product or service is that you will quickly lose that customer the minute someone else beats you. And someone will eventually beat your price. A better strategy is to be ready when someone tells you that your price is too high. Be ready by knowing how you will respond. You may want to ask if the carrier they have been quoted is an A rated carrier. You may want to ask what limits of coverage they have been quoted. This may be a good time to use the Feel, Felt, Found approach. What? You don't know about the Feel, Felt, Found strategy? You are going to love this one. Here's how it might work with the price objection. You say "I completely understand how you FEEL Mr. Prospect. I have a lot of great customers who FELT that way at one time. What we have FOUND over time is that a cheap product or service is, more often than not, inferior in quality to products and services whose investment might be just a little more. We work hard to make sure our customers have the best value which means the best coverages and a fair price. Is this how you feel about most of your important financial decisions as well Mr. Prospect?" The bottom line here Jenna is to let the customer know you understand how they are feeling right now and that you have worked with many customers who were right where they are now. Then, show them how your experience in this area has convinced you that cheap is not always best and make a kind attempt to get them to say yes to you.

You need to be passionate about what you're selling

You can't sell what you don't believe in. If you are someone who believes insurance is a racket or that insurance is a gamble, then you should get another job. When someone refers to insurance as a racket, they are using that term as meaning a scam or swindle. Of course, insurance is not a scam. When you pay insurance premiums with the promise from the carrier that they will pay for the repairs or replacement of whatever gets damaged by the perils insured against, they really will pay. It's a legal contract, not a scam.

But, to be exceptional at selling insurance, you must not only believe that it is a product people need, you must also be passionate about the process of helping more and more people be insured and insured properly. When you love doing something, you will work at it harder and your enthusiasm will influence others to want to do business with you.

Take advantage of sales automation

Like I have said before, automate everything you can. With sales, that may be having an automatic email generate from your agency management system after you provide a quote. It may be the use of electronic signature technology to enable an easy remote transaction. It could be the ability to accept credit cards and checks by phone through your agency management system to make buying insurance from you easy.

What you pay attention to gets results

In life, you may find that you seem to phase in and out of things you are interested in and are paying attention to. This is true outside of work as well as in your work life. Personally, you may do great for a few days, weeks, or months doing things that are important to you like reading daily spiritual devotionals, exercising, or doing something a little extra for those close to you. At work, you may do well for a while at putting in the needed hours each week, reading books for self-improvement, or saying thank you often to team members. Then, you skip a day, or a week, or a month doing that thing that you thought had become a habit. You then may go days, weeks, or months not focused or even thinking about that habit. At some point, if that habit was producing results, you will notice its absence. For example, if spending a few minutes each day on devotionals or meditation had increased your level of peace and calmness, then when you stop, there will be a point when you notice that you have become less at peace each day and are more anxious. If you stop exercising, you will start to notice that you don't have as much energy and you have put on a few pounds.

My point here is that when your situation is not to your liking, all you have to do is make it a focus and pay attention to it for a while. When you ignore finances, they normally decline. When you ignore personal or work relationships, they normally decline. When you ignore sales numbers, they normally decline.

The best way to stay focused on an area like sales is to schedule weekly or monthly meetings. As with marketing, meetings force you to revisit and review numbers regularly and make changes to action steps as needed to continue moving towards your goals.

Seven touches

It's easy to talk yourself into not wanting to "bother" your prospect. However, in my experience, if you are kind and persistent, you will have more success than if you are kind and give up quickly.

I have heard that seven follow up attempts is the magic number so let's go with that for now. Let's say someone calls you to get a quote and you tell them the coverage you recommend along with the price. If they tell you they will check around a little more, remind them you have shopped this with many companies for them and this is the best coverage and price combination you have come up with. If you are not successful in making them a customer today, you will need to follow up.

If you follow up once the following day or week and you leave them a message, send them an email, or even talk to them, and they tell you they have not decided yet who they will be using to insured this car, home, or business with, let them know you would love to work with them and then ask them for their business. People more often appreciate you caring about them than they are aggravated or offended. If they don't buy today, you should suspense a follow-up.

My point here is mostly that people are busy these days and they will very often not buy today because they don't have time to make the decision. If you follow up daily, twice a week, or weekly and use a combination of emails and phone calls, and do this up to seven times before you give up, you will end up serving more people than if you give up quickly.

Key Takeaways

- Define your sales goals.

- Track and improve the team's performance.

- Account rounding and cross-selling

- To incentivize or not to incentivize

- Implement an ongoing training plan.

- Meet with the sales team.

- Treat everyone with kindness.

- Close deals over the phone.

- You can't sell what you don't believe in.

- You need to be passionate about what you are selling.

- Take advantage of sales automation.

- What you pay attention to gets results.

- Seven touches

Suggested Reading

- Sell Your Way To The Top by Zig Ziglar

- Spin Selling by Neil Rackham

- Advanced Selling Strategies by Brian Tracy

- The Ultimate Sales Machine by Chet Holmes

Action Steps

- Schedule training.

- Schedule sales meetings.

- Give at least one compliment today.

CHAPTER **6**

CUSTOMER SERVICE

"There is only one boss - The Customer. They can fire everybody in the company from the chairman on down simply by spending their money somewhere else."
—Sam Walton

"Just having satisfied customers isn't good enough anymore. If you really want a booming business, you have to create raving fans."
—Ken Blanchard

"Your most unhappy customers are your greatest source of learning."
—Bill Gates

"The key is when a customer walks away, thinking 'Wow, I love doing business with them, and I want to tell others about the experience.'"
—Shep Hyken

"People do not care how much you know until they know how much you care."
—Teddy Roosevelt

"Customer service should not be a department. It should be the entire company."
—Tony Hsieh

"The sole reason we are in business is to make life less difficult for our clients"
—Matt Odgers

"People will forget what you said. They will forget what you did. But they will never forget how you made them feel."
—Maya Angelou

I love talking about customer service. Having a successful business of any type requires several things working well together like finance, leadership, marketing, sales, human resources and last but not least, customer service. At Jenesis, we toss in development which doesn't really exist in an insurance agency unless you consider it the process of finding the right carriers, convincing them to let you represent them, and keeping them happy. Let's begin with our desired outcome—Our Goals.

Define the desired customer service experience

Jenna, do you remember when you were little? How much did we love Disney World? For that matter, just think about how much we love Disney World now. What is it that we love so much? Is it the fact that it's so clean? Is it because they have music playing everywhere you go? Is it because they have cool attractions and rides? Or, could a part of why we like Disney World so much be because of the way we feel when we are there? Maya Angelou once said, "People will forget what you said. They will forget what you did. But they will never forget how you made them feel."

I think it's important to look around us and always be aware as we experience customer service and life and what we identify as good and bad customer service. We all have had experiences where the customer service is exceptional and we were pretty blown away. The cool extra effort someone gives when helping us goes a long way. We all have also experienced ridiculously bad customer service.

Before you can really establish a customer service plan, which of course we need to have in writing just like our marketing and sales plans, we must first define what we want our customer service to be like. Just like we share our mission with our team, we need to also share our thoughts about what we want our customers to experience.

How do you get people to care as much as you?

It all begins with you! Your team will care as much about your customers as you care about your team. This one took me a long time to really understand and embrace. I always felt like I was fair and caring to my team, but over the years I've improved at truly trying to help them and place my focus there. This allows them, in turn, to put their focus on the customer. We talked about how to treat your team when we discussed leadership, and we will do it again when we discuss human resources. It is so important that I want to touch on it here as well. You must select the right people for your team, help them become successful, treat them with kindness and respect, and be clear about your expectations. When the right people are well trained and cared for, they will exceed your customer's expectations.

Who do you do business with that impresses you?

Do you remember, Jenna, how impressed you were when we started noticing what amazing customer service Chick-fil-A offered? It was not just "My pleasure!" It was everything! It was the fact that at a fast food restaurant during busy times when you pulled up to the drive-thru, team members were standing there to help you through that process to speed things up. And not only were they there in body, but they were also very aware and intentional about the experience you were about to have. They, of course, got your name. All the team members you would talk to in the next few minutes of that process would call you by name. Using a customer's name is huge. I believe that anyone's favorite word is probably their own name. If you happen to have dined in at a Chick-fil-A, after you placed your order you would take a seat and someone would bring your order out to you. This art of customer service was not common in the fast food world and it probably seemed excessive compared to what's "good enough," by most people's standards.

Greet customers at the door

Jenna, think about most insurance agencies you've visited. When you walk in the door and agents are sitting behind a desk, do they sit there and say hello and wave you over to them? Or, do they stand up, possibly even walk around the desk for you, and greet you face-to-face with a smile? Think for a moment about the difference between the two experiences. Which one might make the customer feel special and important? Now, some agents will say things like, "Well, that's just too much," or "My customers would be uncomfortable if I walked over and opened the door for them." I believe that's the way the other fast food restaurants felt, while Chick-fil-A team members were greeting customers at the drive-thru, serving their meal at their table, all while saying it was their pleasure to do it.

Choose your words carefully

If you pull up a customer's account in your system and notice their policy is canceled, do not blurt out "Your policy has canceled." That may terrify your customer. You may be thinking to yourself that this can easily be fixed, but your customer may not know that. Start out your conversation a little easier like, "It looks like your policy may have recently canceled, so let me take a look to see what we need to do to reinstate your coverage." See the difference?

If a customer becomes unhappy because their policy canceled at 12:01 AM this morning and they assumed they had coverage the rest of the day, don't just say "that's how it works and it's always worked that way." Say something like, "I completely understand why you thought your coverage would have ended at the end of today and not at the beginning. Everyone is surprised about how that works. Let me take a look to see what our options are." By the way, see how I said, "our" options and not "their" options? That's huge.

We have already discussed referrals when we talked about marketing and again when we talked about sales. Now, let's talk about it yet again. Referrals are the best source of new customers and providing amazing customer service is the best way to get more referrals.

When you take a look at your source reports each month, your goal should be to have referrals at the top. The cool thing about focusing on getting referrals as your top new business source is that at the same time you are doing that, you are improving retention by creating an amazing customer experience.

Track and optimize the customer experience

So, how do you know if you're doing a good job or not? Retention and referrals are the two best indicators of the kind of service you are providing your customers. If you do not track your retention, you'll have no clue where you stand on keeping customers. For example, 95% retention is great but it would still be fun to try to improve it. 75% retention is bad and you must work hard to improve that. Track and monitor your referrals and have a plan for getting more and more referrals.

In addition to monitoring retention and referrals as indicators for your customer service, you can also ask your customers to give you a score. We have always asked our customers how they heard about us. And, if it's a referral, we have also asked the name of the person who referred them. In addition, we track that information in our agency management system and believe it's important to always thank the person who sent us the referral. It's easy in our agency management system, and probably in most agency management systems, to have automatic direct mail, email, and/or text message sent to our customers and prospects for a variety of reasons. This is a great way to ask the customer's opinions of your service. When new customers get an automated email from your agency saying "Thank you for becoming a customer," that's a great time to not only tell them about the other services you offer but to ask them for referrals. It's also an excellent time to ask them to score their experience buying insurance from you. If you track the score, it will not take long for you to determine your average score. Once you know your average score, you can start making changes and monitor the score to make sure the changes you are making are working. You can do the same thing for renewing customers as a part of your retention plan. Use automated emails, direct mail, and/or text messages to your current customers to notify them of upcoming renewals, payments due, etc. and include a customer survey from time to time asking how you are doing.

Net Promoter Score (NPS)

I have been reading a lot over the last few years about the Net Promoter Score or NPS. I have not used it in the past but have plans to implement it into Jenesis soon. Here is my view of how it works.

You send an email to your existing clients asking them one simple question. That question is, "How likely are you to recommend us to others?" Ask them to respond on a scale from 1 to 10 with 1 being very unlikely and 10 being very likely. If they respond with a 9 or 10, you should note that in your software to know who those people are. You should also thank them and ask if they would be willing to give you an online review on any of the sites that might help you. Give them the links to the sites and remind them they can copy and paste from one to the other to make it easy for them.

If they respond with a 1-6, email them back or call them if possible, and ask what you could do to improve the experience they are having with you. For this part, take it seriously and do all you can to make needed changes.

The 1-6 group is called detractors, the 7 and 8's are called passives, and the 9 and 10's are called promoters.

To calculate your NPS, subtract the percentage of detractors from the percentage of promoters. For example, if 40% of those who respond are promotors and 20% are detractors, you will subtract 20 from 40 to get a NPS of 20.

Once you have your score, don't spend too much time worrying about what your NPS score "should" be or how it should be compared to your competitors. Get to work to improve your score and don't waste your time with others except to learn what they might be doing better than you.

Use automation to improve the customer experience

You should have systems in place to automatically send texts, emails, and/or direct mail, strategically to prospects you have quoted but not yet written, new customers, those who have sent you a referral, customers who have left you, and the list goes on. Invest the time to put these processes in place; then, move on to working on other things while this happens every day automatically.

Do anything that may improve the customer experience. You should accept credit cards and checks over the phone, rather than requiring a customer to come in. You should also offer an electronic signature option. Accepting credit cards, checks by phone and offering an electronic signature option for your customers allows them to do business with you without the inconvenience of being forced to come to your office.

You should also suggest ACH payments to all customers. From the standpoint of retention and convenience for both you and the customer, having their payments drafted from their account automatically by the carrier is a win-win-win.

Make sure you have a chat option on your website and make sure your sales team is available to engage with customers and prospects. This is growing in popularity as are chatbots, and I am excited to see where this goes in the future.

Answer the phones always and quickly

I have spent a lot of time at many insurance agencies. I have had the privilege to watch and learn from some of the best. Agencies who have the largest teams and who serve the most customers always answer incoming calls and do not let them go to voicemail. They also answer them quickly and with a standard phrase. They never say "hold please" and put the caller on hold but they get their permission to put them on hold. They are pleasant to the caller even before they know if it's a customer, prospect, or telemarketer. Now, you may say that's easy for an agency with a large team. What about those agencies with just two or three staff members or a one-person startup? I agree that a smaller staff may present a challenge if you are with a customer and a call comes in. My point is to work hard to answer the phone quickly and in a way that makes the caller happy to be speaking with you. I have been in agencies when the phone rang, the staff continued their personal conversations with each other and let the phone ring several times while they finished talking about something that could have waited. This makes me cringe. One thing I want to add about talking on the phone is to always smile. A smiling person sounds like a happy person. I was wrong—I have one more thing while we are talking about phone customer service. Did you see how I did that? I admitted when I was wrong. If you are wrong, admit it. Another huge communication trick is knowing that the tone of your voice is more important than the words you choose. If you smile, that will help. Give thought to your tone and energy. Something simple like, "I will do what I can to help you" said without energy is so different than, "I will do what I can to help you" with energy. Try it now. Consider a few changes like, "I will do what I 'can' to help you," where you emphasize the 'can' may sound negative, whereas "I 'will' do what I can to help you," where you emphasize the 'will' may sound like you are going to bat for the customer.

Return calls and emails

There will be times when you don't return a phone call or email as quickly as you should or even don't do it at all. The reasons for this are normally because you dread it for some reason, you are just too busy, you don't feel it's important, you completely forget, or you never got the message, voice mail or email because of human or technical error.

You will become known as someone who is dependable and returns calls and emails, or you will become known as someone who is unreliable and doesn't respond. I recommend you work hard to become the first.

One trick to help with this is to answer calls when they come in rather than letting them go to voicemail. Listening to them later takes time, as does returning the call. When you return that call, you may or may not connect with the person and you may enter a game of time-wasting phone tag. In my experience, I am glad I answered the call the first time rather than letting it go to voicemail. The only potential advantage of letting a call go to voicemail is that you can listen to the message at your leisure and have time to prepare to return the call if research may be in order. If you know who the caller is, I recommend answering the call.

One major rule here is to always return calls and emails on the same day unless the call or email came in after normal business hours. One way to make sure you do this is to schedule a few minutes at the end of each day to review any outstanding calls or emails from the day. If you are not going to be able to return a call on the same day, at least send an email to let them know you received their message and that you will call them by [give a specific time of day] the next day. Then, make sure you do what you said you would do. It's even better if you give them a quick call, even if it's after normal business hours. If you don't get them but get their voicemail, they may be impressed that you called after hours. Just let them know it was important to you to return their call and you are sorry you missed them. Tell them you will call again tomorrow. Don't put the burden on them to call you back, but let them know you plan to call them again and when they can expect your call. The same is true for returning emails. If you were not able to reply to an email quickly during the day because you were busy or traveling, taking a few minutes at the end of the day or in the evening to reply will show that you care enough about the person to be thinking about them after the workday has ended.

Body language

Studies have proven that people decide how credible you are based on your body language more than the words you use or the tone of your voice. In fact, your words only account for seven percent of your successful communication, your tone and inflection account for thirty-eight percent, while your body language makes up fifty-five percent.

All three components of communication should be considered at all times; however, many people don't give much thought to their body language. In today's world of remote communication, body language is not always relevant. Your body language is not only sending a message to the person on the other side of your desk, but it's also sending a message to your brain. It's worth researching how you can use body language to send a message of caring, trustworthiness, confidence, and empathy. For example, standing rather than sitting makes you feel and appear more confident. Making eye contact and smiling makes you and others feel more engaged.

Listen before providing a solution

It's so easy when others begin to explain their problem to quickly think you know where they are going, so you interrupt them to start explaining the solution. The problem is not that you may be wrong or right, it's how you come across as being disrespectful. It's never a good idea to interrupt anyone. Just be patient and allow the person to finish their story. Sometimes they just want to be heard. After they finish, start by saying something like "I hear what you are saying" or "I think I understand and I am sorry about your situation." Then, use the "active listening" technique of repeating back to them what you understood their problem to be. Most of the time you may be right in your understanding and they will confirm that. Sometimes, however, they may add a little more detail to better explain their real problem.

After you have let them explain their problem, repeat it back to them to make sure you really do understand. Show compassion and concern for them and their problem. Then, you are ready to tell them your thoughts for resolving the problem. People don't care how much you know until they know how much you care.

Sales can happen while providing customer service

While helping existing customers, your team will have a lot of opportunities to help grow the business. I have already mentioned that referrals are the best source of new business. People will recommend their friends and family only if they trust and like your organization. The team providing ongoing support is in the best position to make sure your customers like and trust your organization. If your customers receive average support, then your agency will not be on their mind when it comes to ecommendations to others. However, if your customers love calling or visiting your agency, they will want to share that experience with others. They will want to share that experience for two reasons. One reason is that they want their friends and family to be happy like they are. The second reason is that they will want to help you. When I say "you" here, I am referring to your organization which is you and your team. It's all for one and one for all.

There are other ways the support experience can help grow your agency. One of those ways would be to make sure you are insuring everything your customers have to insure. If you make use of the account rounding tools in your agency management system, it will be easy to remember to verify when you are working with a customer that you have asked them about other lines of business. For example, if you are only insuring their auto, your account rounding tools will remind you to ask about their home or if they own a motorcycle, a second home, a business, etc.

Another way, and there are many, many ways, would be to verify your customer is insured correctly and that they understand the coverage they have. For example, do they really understand what limits of coverage they have? Do they know their personal articles like jewelry may not be covered well on their home policy if they are not scheduled?

Customer service training

Is your support team perfect at providing support? Are they as good as they can possibly be? If there is room for improvement, how can we help them improve? I believe that we all can improve in everything we do. When it comes to customer service, decide how much money and time you have to invest, then decide how you want to provide the training. There are so many options ranging from online programs to local workshops. To get started, keep this simple and have an annual support training plan. As a part of this plan, pick something simple like working with each team member to help them understand the value of ongoing training. It's also important as a part of a training plan for individuals to understand how they learn best. Some people prefer taking a local class, while others may prefer doing something online. Schedule one training event this year for each support team member. This may even be a goal for some of them and give them something to celebrate when they complete it. Remember, when individuals make an effort to learn more, they will learn more, and they will be better for doing it. Your job is to help everyone to be so good that other organizations will want to steal them from you, but you should treat them so well that they never want to leave you.

Sorry, but we can't do that

When a customer asks if you can do something, never immediately say no. Consider their request carefully, think of all options, and make every effort to be flexible and helpful. Do you remember when I said you need to provide a memorable experience? Make sure that experience is a good memory and not a bad one. Also, it's not easy to provide an amazing customer experience, so take advantage of every opportunity possible. When someone asks you to do something you would not normally do, chances are your competitor would not normally do it either. If you can be creative and come up with a way to help the customer, you will be remembered.

If you are unable to do something a customer asks of you and if you are unable to meet them halfway, then choose your words carefully when you respond. Use a tone of voice that indicates you would like to help if possible. Show compassion. If you are face to face with the customer, use body language that shows humility. When providing information that is not in a customer's favor, remember to explain the reason you are unable to accommodate their request. Tell them you wish you could do that thing, and if possible, provide other options given their situation. One way to do this is to ask yourself, "How would I want to be treated in this situation?"

Don't come across as too busy to help

When a customer walks in your office or calls you on the phone, even if you are super busy, never let the customer know that. The customer will not be impressed that everyone needs some of your time. Customers are concerned about what they need. You should make that customer feel like he or she is your only customer. If you do that, you stand a much better chance that customers choose you to be their only insurance agent. As an added benefit, you will likely get referrals from a customer who feels special.

Lead, don't point

Never tell a customer what to do or whom to call. Transfer them instead. Do you like to be told what to do? Nope. No one does. If a customer needs to speak with someone else in your organization, don't just say, "You need to contact Bob because he handles that." Instead, hand off that customer in a way that's proactive. Say, "I am not able to address your issue, but I know who can. I am going to have you speak with Bob. He handles claims and can help you. Is it okay if I transfer you to Bob?" If Bob is unavailable, offer to have Bob contact the customer as soon as he is free. Don't consider the issue resolved until you can confirm that this customer is in someone else's care.

Pace to your customer's tempo

When working with a customer who likes to chat more than you do, they may not "click" with you if you are very direct and to the point. On the other hand, if a customer is in a hurry or is a direct person, they may get annoyed if you want to talk about the weather. Be aware of your customer's temperament and match it with your own personal style. When I was helping someone much older than me and very proper, I would be on my best grammatical behavior and call them sir or mam. When I was helping someone younger and less formal, I would relax a little and be more casual. This works in all areas of life, not just customer service.

Is there anything else I can help you with?

Never end a conversation with a customer without asking if there is anything else you can do to help them. Also, when ending a conversation, make sure you and the customer are on the same page as far as next steps. If there are additional steps needed to resolve a question or problem for the customer, you will always want to let them know what you are planning to do and when they can expect to hear from you. Then you can say, "Other than that, is there anything else I can do for you?" If you believe you have resolved the question or problem and that there are no further steps, you can confirm that by saying something like, "So Mr. Wonderful, have I taken care of everything you needed today?" If he says yes, you can say, "Great! Is there anything else I can help with today?"

Under promise and over deliver

This phrase has been around a long time. The problem I have with it is, why in the world would you ever under promise? That's setting the bar really low. It makes it easy to be average in the service you provide to your customer. We have already talked about the fact that people have high expectations so being average is really being below average. Ever heard the phrase, "When you are on time, you are late; and when you are early, you are on time?" Same philosophy. A better phrase is **over promise and way over deliver**.

Treat your coworkers as customers

You may have heard this before. Do you know what it means? I think the real value in viewing your team like you do customers is that you are respectful and helpful toward your coworkers like you are toward your customers. Why does this matter? It matters because these are the people you work with every day. It's the people you need to unite with to accomplish great work together. Your team needs to be a well oiled, finely tuned machine and being respectful and helpful is the oil and tuning needed. Too often, we treat our coworkers differently than our customers. We put customers first and coworkers last. Don't let this concept get complicated. You may say that customers are more important because if it were not for customers, none of you would have a job. But my philosophy is that if it were not for the team, you would not have any customers. It's a two-way street. Just be safe, respect and help EVERYONE.

Sometimes you must fire a customer

I am all about going the extra mile and providing amazing customer service. But, it's possible to have a particular customer that is not worth having. Be careful with this because I am not giving you a license to fire every other customer. What I am saying here is that if you have one customer that is disrespectful to your team, uses profanity when speaking with them, does not seem to appreciate what anyone does, takes up a great deal of time, and is just plain difficult to work with, it may be better to send them a nice letter to say you feel his/her needs will be better met somewhere else.

This is really hard to do and no fun for sure. But, it is most likely better than keeping a customer who is not happy with your organization and who is making you and your team miserable. If you have too many of these customers, you may want to consider taking a hard look in the mirror because the problem may not be with them. In my lifetime, I have done this less than a handful of times.

Key Takeaways

- How do you get people to care as much as you?

- Who do you do business with that impresses you?

- Greet customers at the door.

- Choose your words carefully.

- Use automation to improve the customer experience.

- Do anything that may improve customer experience.

- Answer the phones always and quickly.

- Smile.

- Be aware of your tone of voice and body language.

- Return calls and emails.

- Listen and let your customer finish before providing a solution.

- Sales can happen while providing customer service.

- Customer service team needs ongoing training.

- Sorry, but we can't do that: Be flexible and helpful.

- Don't come across as too busy to help.

- Never tell a customer what to do or whom to call. Be proactive in getting them to the right place.

- Pace to your customer's tempo.

- Ask if there is anything else you can do to help.

- Over promise and way over deliver.

- Treat your coworkers as customers.

- Sometimes you must fire a customer.

Suggested Reading

- Customer Mania! by Ken Blanchard

- Delivering Happiness by Tony Hsieh

Action Steps

- Develop a customer service training plan.

- Schedule customer service training.

- Make a list of your worst customer service experiences and what made them bad.

- Make a list of your best customer service experiences and what made them great.

- Create a process to measure retention and referrals. Evaluate the support team. How they handle calls and customers who come in the office.

- Create a way to evaluate how team members service each other.

CHAPTER 7

HUMAN RESOURCES

"There are only three measurements that tell you nearly everything you need to know about your organization's overall performance: employee engagement, customer satisfaction, and cash flow. It goes without saying that no company, small or large, can win over the long run without energized employees who believe in the mission and understand how to achieve it."
—Jack Welch, former CEO of GE

"Train people well enough so they can leave, treat them well enough so they don't want to."
—Richard Branson

Jenna, there are four items that I'd like to share with you about building your dream team. There is absolutely nothing as important as the people you work with. It is very important that you:

1. Understand the principles of recruiting and hiring the right people.
2. Invest time and money to properly train your team during the onboarding phase and forever.
3. Be interested in each team member.
4. Celebrate successes.

Recruit and hire the right people

Let's start at the beginning. The beginning is when you decide you would like to add someone to your team. How do you know when it's time? This is tricky because, on one hand, you could say that you should be able to afford and have a need for an additional team member. When your business is small, that's difficult. The reason it's difficult is that you most often will need someone before you can afford them. Also, what if you have someone suddenly leave the team? Even with a two-week customary notice, you will not likely find a perfect fit that quickly. The truth is that you should always be involved in scouting talent. If you have a few possibilities in mind, then when you have the need and the funds to bring someone on, you will not make a quick, often bad, choice. Here is another concept that complicates things a bit. If you wait until you "need" to hire someone, either because someone left or because you have grown, then you most likely have been suffering at least a little for a while. Here is what I mean. If you have been growing and have now gotten to the point that you need to add someone to the team, then I bet you have been providing less than amazing customer service and your current team members most likely have been feeling somewhat overwhelmed for a while. So, how do you prevent this? You make the decision to add to your team, either before you need that person or at least in the early phase of needing them. In my experience, when I have added someone in any capacity, when it is the right person, it has always improved the overall health of the organization from morale to finances.

Hiring

Let's now talk about the hiring process. Hiring is completely different than recruiting. Recruiting is the process of scouting and getting people to agree to an interview. Hiring is the part where you go through the interview and make an offer.

Hopefully, you have narrowed the candidates down to ones with the talent, skill, attitude and work ethic that will fit with your team.

Remember, you can train for skill so hire for attitude. When you get close to making an offer, be sure to do background checks on the candidates. I did not do that for the first twenty years of my career and paid for it several times. I am not talking about checking references, though you should do that too, I am talking about a legal background check. Most people are perfectly fine with this and understand it is just part of the process. The cost is almost nothing to do this.

You should have a hiring checklist. As a matter of fact, you should have a checklist for everything. When I got my pilot's license in 2007, I learned on day one that using a checklist was not an option. People die in aviation when routine details are overlooked. You may not die if you hire someone and forget to tell them you only pay monthly rather than weekly, but you never want your new team members to be surprised.

Training, coaching, and leading

Your job as a leader is to build other leaders. Your job is to be careful not to spend too much time doing, but rather more time helping and coaching others. Most anything you find yourself doing, you need to be teaching others how to do it. People will do great work if they feel appreciated and feel like they are making a difference. At some point, you will have someone on your team that doesn't belong on your team. It may not even be their fault. It may just be that this is not the right place or the right work for them to be doing. If you keep them around when they shouldn't be there, you're not doing anybody any favors. They need to be where they should be. There's a question that asks, "How do you know when it's the right time to part ways with a team member?" And the answer to that question according to the saying is, "You are ready to part ways when you first think about it." So in other words, if you start thinking too much about whether someone is a good fit or not, they probably are not. For people who are happy, doing great work and getting satisfaction with your team, it will never cross your mind to wonder if this person is the right fit.

It can be challenging to set aside time for training and to figure out where and how the training will be done. Udemy.com is one example of a training platform, but there are many and it's worth time to research what works best for you. I feel like a good mixture of online training and classroom programs produce the best result.

Be interested in each team member

Remember, it's better to be interested than to be interesting. Your job is to make other people successful. Most leaders would give anything if the people who work for them would care as much about the business as they do. They would give anything that is except to change the way they lead. You will get absolutely nothing from impressing your team. However, you will get a ton of value from not only showing that you care, but by being interested in each member of your team. You should know about their families, hobbies, and what's important in life and work to them. You don't have to interrogate them to get this information and as a matter of fact, you don't have to get it all at once. You never learn everything about anyone all at once. Even your best friend didn't start out as your best friend and you didn't learn everything about them at your first meeting. Take your time but just remember to be aware of the importance of being interested in others. People will like you more because you like them, rather than because you have done great things.

Celebrate successes

This is so important it needs to be repeated here. I know we have already discussed it but we also discussed spaced repetition. See what I am doing here?

If you "test" people by allowing them to figure out things on their own or waiting until they complete a big project, then show appreciation, you will have fewer celebrations and fewer successfully completed projects. If, however, you show interest, pay attention, and celebrate small accomplishments along the way, you will make people happy and encourage them to keep going and successfully finish the big task.

Celebrate in many ways. I like posting on our internal social media site for other team members to see. I also like sending a personal email, giving them a phone call, or even sending a gift card as a way of saying "good job."

Redundancy in people

We have talked about this already too but, remember, repetition is required for effective learning so I am applying what I preach here.

Just like it's important to have backups in place when it comes to hardware and software, it's even more important when it comes to your team. If there is any job that only one person knows how to do, it, you may have a problem on your hands when that person is on vacation, out sick, or wins the lottery. On your job descriptions next to each task that someone does, add the name or names of who else can do that task. I would go one step further. When someone knows how to do that thing really well because they have been doing it for a long time, give it to someone else to do for a while. If the person who knows it well is needed to take it back, they will know it well enough to do that. But, if you only train someone else on that activity to be a backup if needed, they may struggle when called on.

Another advantage of having more than one person know how to do everything is that when others are trained on that job, the person doing the training will be forced to teach and like they say, to teach is to learn twice. During the process of teaching, they may rethink how it's done and possibly come up with improvements to the process. Also, the person being taught will often ask great questions and those questions may lead to improvements. Finally, after the new person does the job for a while, they are likely to have ideas that will improve the process.

Say thank you a LOT

How often should you say thank you? Is there a rule of thumb? Should it be a goal to tell each person "thank you" at least once a day? The answer to this question is that the "rule" is to say "thank you" EVERY time you have an opportunity. For the people you work closely with, if you don't have an opportunity every day, something is wrong. You need to also coach your team to treat each other this way. Each time you ask someone to call a customer for you and they agree, say "thank you." When they let you know later they talked with the customer and everything has been done, say "thank you." You can create opportunities to say "thank you" by asking someone to do an important task for you. You can look for opportunities and I think you will find lots of them.

Be transparent

If you start a business from scratch, it's not easy to hire people who care as much as you do. You should be comfortable with that and not let that be your goal. A better goal is to bring good people into your organization, treat them with great respect, and help them be successful. When you partner with the right people, treat them well, and help them be successful, they are more likely to be happy and fulfilled. When people are happy and fulfilled in a job, they do great work. That's really what you are looking for. You want to work with great people who enjoy what they do, enjoy the customers, enjoy their team, and care about the quality of the work they do.

To accomplish all of this, you must be transparent. Never play games with people. When you work with the right people, you are able to be transparent, share why we do what we do, and what result we are looking for this week, month, quarter, year and beyond.

Compensation

Compensation is not a four letter word. So many employers and employees are not comfortable talking about money. Again, when you have partnered with the right people, conversations like this should be easy. When you offer someone a job, you tell them how much they will be paid and they agree to take the job or not. After that is where most employers and employees stop talking about the money plan. Will they get a raise every year? How much is the average raise? If the answer to these questions might be, "well it depends," then be clear about what it depends on.

I think how much you offer to pay someone to partner with you is a function of the job, the area of the country where you live, the work environment, the experience of the candidate, and the pool of applicants. I think how much of a raise you give people over time is a function of the same things plus how much the company is growing and how they affected that growth.

If you are transparent with each team member, they will always know where you stand with their performance and if they reciprocate that transparency, you will always know their level of satisfaction with the work they do and how they are compensated.

Incentives and bonuses

Should you provide individual incentives for performance? If you want to encourage individuals to work alone and for themselves, then yes. If, however, you want to encourage individuals to work as a team, then only provide a team bonus based on company growth. If you have one team member who is a superstar performer so you think you need to compensate them differently than those who contribute less to the overall success of the company, then adjust their salary accordingly.

The danger in providing an individual performance incentive is that you encourage people to look out for number one and not look out for the company as a whole. If you have a superstar, that superstar may be able to share knowledge with the team to help the entire organization prosper rather than keeping that knowledge as their personal secret weapon.

Your job as a leader is to take care of your team

As you work with a team for the purpose of solving someone's problem by providing insurance or software, you must make sure you are taking care of the team who is taking care of the customer. One way to do this is to help with retirement planning. You are in this for the long haul and you want good people to stick around for a while. You also care about their well-being and future. Most people will not put money aside for retirement as they should because they don't think they can afford to do it right now and they plan to do it later. For most people, later is too late or never comes.

You should set up a retirement plan where your team can have the option of money being taking from their paychecks and put into a retirement account and they will never even know it's gone. I am not going to get into the difference between qualified and non-qualified plans here because which one is best may be different depending on the situation and opinion. I am also not going to go into the decision to match the employee contribution from the company or not to match. If you can afford to match the first one, two, or three percent, that would be great. If you can't, put that part off until later.

The most important thing is to set up the plan and encourage your team to participate.

Time away policy

People need time away from work. They need to take vacation time to recharge and come back to work happier and with more energy. They need to attend a parent meeting at their kid's school now and then. They may even be sick from time to time.

How much time do you allow people to be away from work? For the first 20 years, I adopted a more traditional vacation/sick day policy. When someone came to work for me, they would "earn" a one week vacation after they worked for me for one year. Then, after five years, they would have earned two weeks. Finally, after working for ten years, they would have earned a whole three weeks of annual vacation time.

As for sick time, we would pay for each person to be sick seven days a year. They qualified for this "benefit" day one.

The result of this plan was that it required a bit of tracking. Also, one interesting fact is that most people were sick seven days a year and of course took the allotted vacation time each year.

About ten years ago, we changed the way we view vacation and sick time. We introduced the "no vacation or sick day policy," which is essentially an unlimited Paid Time Off (PTO) policy. It's not what it sounds like. It means we do not have a policy that regulates vacation or sick time in any way.

People were shocked when we introduced this. Our theory was that if we are working with the right people, they will not abuse the unlimited privilege. The results were AMAZING. Over the last ten years, the average person takes two weeks of vacation time each year and is out two days per year for sickness.

Introducing this policy increased morale and reduced recordkeeping, as well as reduced the number of days people are out each year. The fear of many will be that people will take advantage of them. If they do, they are not the people you want on your team.

Knowing when to part ways

"When people show you who they are, believe them the first time."
--- Dr. Maya Angelou

People seldom change fundamental core behavior characteristics. When you see early signs of problems with attitudes and work ethic, don't hold off too long hoping things will improve. If someone has a great attitude and work ethic, you can help them improve in most other areas. But, when you identify early signs of a bad attitude toward others or the job, it will be unlikely to improve over time.

I have heard it said, the way to know when it's time to part ways with a team member is when you first wonder if you should. There is some truth to this. When a team member is awesome, you would never even consider letting them go.

Another popular phrase is "hire slow and fire fast." This suggests we should take our time and have a comprehensive recruiting and hiring process so we increase the chance we are offering the position to the candidate who is best suited to join the team. It also supports the notion that when you think you may have made a mistake, you should act quickly to rectify the situation.

Some organizations have a policy of terminating ten percent of their employees annually. The concept here is that you will part ways with the ten percent who provide the least value to the organization to make the team stronger. I am not suggesting you have a policy like this. I never have. But, I do think it's a good idea to know who your weakest link is at all times. This may sound negative but it's a valuable exercise. Just ask yourself the question, if someone left today, who would I want it to be in terms of having the least negative effect on the organization? By the way, you should do the same thing in reverse. Who would be the single worst person to leave? If that person left, it would have the greatest negative impact.

Letting someone go is hard. It's the worst thing you will do as a leader. If someone does something terrible, like stealing money, it's not so hard. But, if they are out of work too much, have a less than ideal attitude, or are not performing well, it's a difficult meeting to have. The thing to remember is this. Keeping someone on your team who does not belong is not the right thing for them or for you. If you don't have the guts to set them free now and keep them around for a while longer, then decide to say good bye, you have wasted their time. Letting them stay with you is not a noble move on your part. It's a leadership weakness that most of us suffer from, and by the way, that will negatively impact you, the other team members, and the person you should have been transparent with early on.

Motivation

You need a motivated team. Motivation is like taking a shower. The effects of being motivated do not last long. You need to constantly motivate your team. This can be done by helping them participate in a motivational type of training on a regular basis. It can be done by telling them "thank you" often. It can be done by celebrating them often. It's hard to beat a "job well done" gesture.

Culture

Your organization has a culture. It's up to you to decide if you like it and if not, what you are going to do about it. Culture is one of many trendy terms used over the past few years and it's worth discussion. The culture you create will determine the type of people you work with and the type of customers you work for. A very rigid, structured and straight-laced atmosphere that will work best for people who are comfortable in that atmosphere. If you prefer a more playful environment, those people are a little different. I am not suggesting what your culture needs to be because you need to create a culture that is in alignment with you. If you create a culture that does not match the authentic you, it will be impossible to be happy long term. The culture starts with the leadership and a team built around that culture who matches its style.

Mutual team support

The team members should compliment, congratulate, and encourage each other. Most parents love it when their kids interact well with their siblings. Much in the same way, a leader feels a sense of pride when the team members interact well, support, encourage, and compliment one another. This is something you can be transparent about with each team member. When explaining the reason, the "why," let them know you believe that when they compliment and encourage each other, it improves trust and increases overall team effectiveness. Not to mention that it makes for a happier place to work.

Permission to go back

We talked about this earlier but it's worth another mention. You will find yourself sometimes thinking "I should have …" and when you do, remember that it's ok to have a redo. This can make a big difference in your leadership effectiveness.

Connect the dots

Everyone should really see the connection in what they do with what others do. Much like knowing the "why," knowing the way things connect is a big deal. I have had people swap roles in the past and almost every time, they come away with a new respect for what others do. They often even help come up with better ways of doing things as a result of their new and fresh perspective.

Physical work environment

The space we occupy eight hours a day does matter. The way it looks, the way it feels, the tools used, and even the temperature and lighting matter. Have a nice space that looks good to customers and is a happy place for your team.

Computers

Only the best will do.

Monitors

More is better. No less than two for sure. Also, larger is better so spend the extra money because it's not much more and the average monitor will last several years.

Internet speed

Just like with monitors, more is better. I suggest getting the best available in your area.

Working remotely

Make virtually everyone virtual. Even if most or all of your team need to work in an office accessible to customers, I suggest every team member be set up to work from home when needed. If they can't get to work due to bad weather, a sick kid, or car trouble, it's nice to have the option to still be productive.

Phones

VOIP is best. Shop around for the best fit and price.

Key Takeaways

- Understand the principles of recruiting and hiring the right people.

- Invest time and money to properly train your team during the on-boarding phase and forever.

- Be interested in each team member.

- Celebrate successes.

- Redundancy in people

- Say thank you a LOT.

- Be transparent.

- Compensation: salary, incentives, and bonuses

- Your job as a leader is to take care of your team: ex. retirement planning

- Unlimited time away

- Knowing when to part ways

- Motivation

- Culture

- The team members should compliment, congratulate, and encourage each other.

- Permission to go back

- Everyone should really see the connection in what they do with what others do.

Suggested Reading

- High Five! By Ken Blanchard and Sheldon Bowles

- Gung Ho! By Ken Blanchard and Sheldon Bowles

- The One Minute Manager Builds High Performing Teams by Ken Blanchard

Action Steps

- Schedule your quarterly individual meetings and team meetings.

CHAPTER 8

Conclusion

"I think it's very important to have a feedback loop, where you're constantly thinking about what you've done and how you could be doing it better. I think that's the single best piece of advice: constantly think about how you could be doing things better and questioning yourself."
—Elon Musk, founder of PayPal and Tesla

"People who are truly strong lift others up. People who are truly powerful bring others together."
—Michelle Obama, attorney and former First Lady of the United States

"The challenge of leadership is to be strong, but not rude; be kind, but not weak; be bold, but not bully; be thoughtful, but not lazy; be humble, but not timid; be proud, but not arrogant; have humor but without folly."
—Jim Rohn, entrepreneur and motivational speaker

Everything fits together like a puzzle. Leadership, finance, marketing, sale, and customer service.

Running a business is like playing the mole-in-the-hole carnival game. When one area is running smoothly, you will often experience a problem in another area. When you turn your attention to that area to resolve the problem, another one will pop up somewhere else. If you expect your experience to be perfect, you will be disappointed. When you expect it to be a constant game of problem-solving and making adjustments, you will be better equipped to survive.

I want to finish up with some reflection on principles we have already discussed, but I also want to share a few general thoughts and principles I believe affect success and happiness in business as well as in life.

You can't do it all

Knowing what and whom to say no to is more important than saying yes. If we allow too much to gather on our to-do list, we will be unable to focus on doing the right things well. If you feel you currently have too much on your plate, take a time-out to write down your complete list, then divide it into two parts. One part will be what's VERY important, and the other part will be what's not so important. Then, with the important part, try to delegate what you can to others on your team or even outsource some of them. This will go a long way in clearing your mind and allowing you to focus on what you enjoy and what will have the greatest impact.

Closely related to the concept of overload is the idea that there is so much information out there and so many competing priorities for your time, it can get confusing. For example, there are more books I want to read than time will allow unless I were to read day and night. There are more marketing possibilities than I can process in my small brain. You simply can't do everything. No successful person has done everything. You must decide, what's most important, what you enjoy doing, what you can afford to invest in, what can be delegated and outsourced, then make your best decision on what to commit to.

Improve your strengths

There are some things you enjoy doing and some things you dislike doing. There are things you seem to be naturally good at and things you seem to struggle with. We are all this way. For many years, my thought was we should work to improve what we are not good at. Let's think about this for a moment. Earlier we talked about people like Bill Gates, Michael Jordan, and Garth Brooks being successful. There is no question they were very good at what they became well known for doing like software, basketball, and music. But what about things they were not so good at? We really don't know what those things might have been because they were not famous for those things. What if Bill Gates identified at an early age that he was just not good at sports. He might have spent a lot of time trying to improve his atheticism. If he had done that, he would not have spent so much time in the computer lab and Microsoft may have never been born or worst of all, he would have been good but not great at building software and may have been a little better but probably not even "good" in sports. When Michael Jordan and Garth Brooks realized they loved basketball and music respectively, they pursued them with full focus and did everything they could to improve.

I tell you this because when you find yourself procrastinating on something, consider delegating or outsourcing it. When you find yourself spending a lot of time on something because it's fun to you, even if those around you can't understand why in the world you enjoy it, this may be your area of strength and may be worth investing in ways to keep getting better at doing it.

Do the dreaded things first

When you have a number of things to do, it's tempting to knock out a few of the easy ones first because it's satisfying to check things off your list. The problem with this is you are likely to keep doing the easy things and continue putting off the hard thing. You will always have new "things" added to your list, so you may keep pushing the hard things further down.

If you will tackle the hard things first, your sense of accomplishment will be much greater than finishing a few easy tasks. The longer you put anything off, the more complicated it seems to become. You forget what you knew about it originally and you have to start from scratch to catch up to where you were with understanding what needs to be done.

Rest to recharge

When you love what you do or when you are so driven to succeed, it's easy to work too much. You don't feel like it's work so the time will fly by. This is often called "being in the zone."

Being in the zone and having a good time with what you are doing is great. However, it's important to keep things in perspective. Working eight to ten hours per day is reasonable. Even working six days a week is not too absurd. However, when you find yourself working more than ten hours daily, for six or seven days a week, for months in a row, you may be heading for burnout.

Taking time each day to completely get away from work is critical to your ability to continue to do great things and be creative. You know Jenna that I am a big believer in hobbies, adventure, and having fun. For me, finding something like getting my pilot's license gave me something that was hard enough to require my full attention, but so different from my day job, it allowed me to completely recharge. You should find ways to recharge often and completely.

You will have seasons of no passion

If you are like me, and I think you are, you will have periods of time when you are hitting on all cylinders and are super passionate about changing the world. Then, there will be times when you just don't seem to have the energy to work or sometimes even enjoy life in general.

Going through these periods of time is completely normal for everyone, especially for an entrepreneur. We all have different cycles as well. For me, I normally have complete passion, energy, and creativity for a few months at a time. Then, I find myself uninterested for a few weeks or sometimes a few months. When things are going great, I seem to have high energy and passion, but when a few things go wrong, my energy and passion seem to decline.

Your cycle may be completely different. You may only experience this lack of passion for a few hours or days at a time. Your cycle may come more or less often than mine. The important thing is to know first is how to identify it, and secondly, what to do about it.

For me, there have been times when I felt tired as a result of working really hard for a few days. When this was the problem, I crashed on the couch for a few hours watching useless but fun television. That seemed to completely recharge my body and mind. Other times, I felt tired and lost passion as a result of complete focus for a few months. This required a little more time away to recharge. At times I may need a long weekend or even a week of vacation. These two types of fatigue, mental and physical fatigue, seem to happen to me a handful of times most years. Now, I sometimes experience another cycle. About every five years, I seem to have a larger loss of passion and greater reduction in my ability to focus. During these times, I decided to buy or sell an agency, get my pilot's license, or out of the blue sign up for guitar, keyboard, or drum lessons. This may not happen to you. This may be unique to me. I still want you to be aware just in case you experience it. These times required a bit more to recharge. By the way, you know when you have recharged because you begin feeling excited about things again. You start having creative, innovative ideas. And, you start having fun when you are hard at work.

The bottom line is to acknowledge how you are feeling and accept that your feelings are normal. Rest, pray, and rejuvenate. Your interest will resurface again and you can push yourself to get back in the game. When you accept your feelings and understand your physical, mental, and emotional needs, magical things begin to happen.

Create adventure

All work and no play make Jack a dull boy. This is a proverb I have heard all my life, but do not know its origin. It means you should not work all the time. I have addressed this already, but I want to repeat it again to emphasize its importance. We all want to be happy in life. Different things make people happy. You have to figure out the thing or things that make you happy every day. I love adventure. I love flying an airplane, being captain of a large boat, riding a motorcycle, and I find it an adventure to build a business. Give consideration to the things that make you happy. It is hard for me to imagine that someone doesn't want adventure in their life.

Love everyone

When I was in middle and high school, I said a prayer most nights. I added to my prayer at about that age, to please let me love everyone. I have no idea why I started praying for that every night. Looking back now, what I like about it is that it was so much better than praying that everyone would love me. It's also much better than asking to be liked or for me to "like" everyone. Love is an entirely different thing altogether. At some point during those years, I started to notice that I had GREAT relationships with MANY people. People didn't irritate me. People seemed to be nice to me all the time.

I encourage you to be aware of the importance of loving everyone. You are connected to EVERYONE in the universe. Never say you "hate" anyone. Always speak positively about people. Give people the benefit of the doubt. Smile and look for ways to help people.

Return the cart at the grocery store for someone. Let someone in front of you when checking out who has fewer items than you. Be interested in others. Ask questions. If this doesn't come naturally for you, try praying for it sincerely and notice what changes.

Don't worry at night

I have found this to be something people experience as they get older. It's not uncommon for adults to have trouble going to sleep or to wake up in the middle of the night with things on their mind. Sometimes it's many things. It may be business or personal finances, relationships, or health. Worries are often rooted in fear. Most of the time, what we worry about never happens. Most of us have spent more time worrying about things that never happen than things that do. Think of FEAR as an acronym for False Evidence Appearing Real.

If you have trouble falling asleep and you have a bad feeling that you are going to lay there for hours or possibly all night, get out of bed. Go somewhere comfortable like the couch, make sure you are warm and comfortable, and read a book that makes you happy and relaxed. Do not think about work. Do not watch television. Keep the lighting dim in the room. Most likely, you will become sleepy within an hour.

You can do the same thing if you wake up in the middle of the night and lay there for a few minutes. You should get up when you start becoming anxious and believe you will not be able to go back to sleep quickly.

The pattern of thought is that it normally starts with one concern then quickly goes to another, then another. Most often the original concern resurfaces and you then go through them all again. The reason counting sheep was something commonly referred to years ago was that it was a strategy to get your mind out of the doom and gloom cycle. Problems seem magnified at night. Just know that if this happens to you now and again, it's normal.

Relax

I have discussed the importance of a good morning routine to help get your day started in the best way possible. If you follow your morning routine, you should be starting your day in a relaxed frame of mind. Being relaxed will allow your brain to be creative and clear.

It's common, however, to allow the circumstances and events of the day to create anxiety. When this happens, we normally do not make the best choices. When you feel yourself losing the relaxed state of mind, take a moment to regroup. Take a deep breath. Go for a walk. Do what works for you to become centered and settled. You will then be better able to move forward with your day.

You may hear people say they do their best work under pressure. I am not going to presume what's best for all people, but I can tell you that most of us normally do not make the best choices when under pressure. I have been stopped way too many times over the years for speeding. Every single time, the officer has taken his or her time to get out of the car. They walked slowly to my car and spoke in a calm and relaxed tone. They came across as having it together and being in complete control. If they jumped out of their car, ran up to mine, and started yelling and talking really fast, it would freak me out but it would also convey they were out of control and not cool, calm, and collected.

Jim Rohn, author, entrepreneur and speaker, says we are the average of the five people we spend the most time with. I couldn't agree more. We were told as children to be careful about the friends we choose. That was great advice. When you think about the person you want to be, look at others as role models. Those role models maybe someone you know or just someone you know of. They may be someone who is now alive or someone who is no longer with us. It's likely you will have more than one role model and that your role models change over the years.

I am not suggesting you work to become someone else. I am suggesting the opposite. You should be yourself. You should be authentic. However, you may change over time. Also, if we do not look to role models for inspiration, we may not uncover the things about ourselves that are hidden and when found, will change our lives.

The reason I have added role models into this five friends concept is this. Your friends should be among your role models. If you are associating with people that you find yourself dreading to be with or find yourself saying negative things about them later, it's critical that you find a way to associate with them less. You are not doing them any favors by blessing them with your presence if it's not a mutually beneficial relationship. Do you remember when we talked about the 80/20 rule? That applies here for sure. You will normally find that a small percentage of your friends give you the most joy. Therefore, you may need to determine if your time is well spent with others.

Consider the distinct areas of your life like relationships, finance, health, work, and spiritually. Make a list of your friends who help you grow in each of those areas. It's not likely or important that any one friend helps you mature in all areas. It's most likely that one or two friends will inspire you to have better relationships because they have had a long, successful, healthy marriage or that they are great at being social. Another friend may motivate you to work hard at your career and to eat well and exercise. I hope you associate with positive, successful, and happy people.

How to make a decision

Nothing may influence the quality of our lives more than the choices we make. Sometimes decisions are really hard. Sometimes we think they are easy, but we still make the wrong choice. Some people simply find it difficult to make any decision at all. To "not" make a decision is a decision, and more times than not, it's the wrong decision.

The best advice I can give you on decision making is this. Think in the future. Think about how you will feel after you make the decision. For example, let's say you are hard at work and it's time for you to exercise. You have a ton of work to do and you are not sure you should stop to exercise. Sometimes, work can be the best excuse ever. Telling yourself or someone else you can't do something because you have to work sounds noble. The truth is most of the time it's just an excuse. We normally do what we "want" to do, and often, exercising is more painful than working. If you stop for a moment and consider how you will feel when you go to bed tonight about your decision, that may help you know which choice is best. If you do not exercise and continue to work, how will you feel about it tonight, tomorrow, next week? If you stop working for an hour to go run or go to the gym, how will you feel after that? I am not going to give you the answer to the dilemma above. The point of this lesson is for you to have a tool that may help you make decisions. The choice you make based on how you will feel later is up to you.

Repetition and consistency is key to learning

I have talked to you a lot about the importance of learning for you and everyone in your organization. It's hard to learn when the learning is spaced out too far and inconsistent. For example, if you wanted to get your insurance license, you would not be as successful if you invested one day a month for five months as you would if you invested one day a week or every day for five days.

Anything worth learning is learned best with frequent repetition. Let me give you another relevant example. If you want to learn how to use a new agency management system and the system is rich with features, it will take a little time to learn. If you work with videos, a manual, or a trainer for one hour per week and are exposed to each feature and workflow only once, it may take you months to truly learn the system well. If, however, you invest one hour per day and have a plan for repeating information two or even three times, you will likely learn more of any system in a few weeks.

Furthermore, you will likely not only just learn the system, but you will also probably master the system.

Because we have always done it that way

The world continues to improve. If we are negative, we will say that the world continues to decline. Let's be positive.

One way things improve is to ask why we do things as we do them? A common response to this question is because we have always done it that way. That's not a good answer.

A newlywed couple was preparing Thanksgiving dinner when the wife asked her husband, who was stuffing the turkey, to cut about one quarter off the end of the turkey. When the husband asked why he should do that, she replied, "I am not sure, that's just how my mom taught me." The young couple decided to call mom to ask why it was necessary to cut off so much of the turkey. When they got mom on the phone and asked the question, she replied," I am not really sure why. That's how your grandma taught me when I was young." Now, everyone was curious why they had been cutting the end of the Thanksgiving turkey for so many years. They finally gave grandma a call and conferenced her in with everyone. The granddaughter asked her, "Grandma, I have always cut off the end of the Thanksgiving turkey because my mom did, and she says she has always done it because you did. Can you tell us why you cut off the end of the Thanksgiving turkey?" The grandma replied, "Well, when your mom was a little girl, the house we lived in had a small oven."

Need I say more? It's healthy to ask why things are done the way they are. There may be good reasons why they were done that way at one point, but circumstances may have changed and there could be a better way today.

Use "and" rather than "but"

I have talked to you about the importance of choosing the right words. Here is one great example of how to do that. It's a little three-letter example and it can be powerful. We can change the way we make people feel simple by using different words.

If you are giving someone feedback and you say something like, "You did a good job with that, but you didn't do that other part," how might that make them feel? What if you said, "You did a great job with that and if you will do that other part, I think you will be all done with that project." Do you see the difference? Be aware of when you use the word "but" and try to replace it with "and" where possible.

Find a few friends to hold you accountable for positive talk

There is no value in speaking negatively. When a customer leaves the office, you should not say, "I am sure glad they are gone because …" or when you get a work assignment, you should not think or say to someone else, "I really dread doing this." What value is there in thinking to say anything negative?

If you don't like the customer and you say something negative after they leave, doesn't that make you experience the negative feeling twice? If you don't like a project you have been assigned and you talk about how much you dread it, does that create more negative energy for you and around the project?

I suggest you play a game with a few close friends and coworkers. Play the "positive words" game. Anytime you say something positive, your close friends will recognize how cool it is that you were positive. If you say something not positive, your friends will mention, but not in front of others, that you are releasing a non-positive vibe into the atmosphere.

I like the old saying, "It is better to not say anything than to say something negative." I think that was intended to reference saying something bad about someone, but I think we should use it in a broader scope.

When we think and speak positive things, we will have more positive things happen to us. When we speak more negative things, we will have more negative things happen. The law of attraction says that if we think something, we increase the chance that it will happen. If you think you will lose a game, gain weight, lose money, etc, you increase the change that will happen. Why not think about speaking about how you will win that game, what you will do when you lose that weight, and what you will do with that extra money?

It's ok to say, "Let me take some time to give that some thought." There will be times when someone will ask you a question that you don't know the answer to at the moment. That's perfectly fine. Don't let the person pressure you into giving them an answer instantly. You may need a little time to consider the question and possibly to research, before you give your answer.

A great response is, "That's a great question. I will give it some thought and get back to you." When you do this, give them a time to expect to hear from you. Depending on the situation, you might tell them you will get back to them in a few minutes or by the end of the day. Or, you may tell them you will get back to them tomorrow or by the end of the week. Also, when that time comes, if you need more time, just let them know you have considered the question and have done some research, but you need just a little more time. Then, be careful and really try to have an answer when you say you will this time. Asking for an extension is fine, but going beyond one extension is seldom great.

Go change the world, you can do this!

I have shared a lot of my thoughts and experiences with you regarding finance, leadership, marketing, sales, customer service, and human resources. Some of what I have shared with you will be helpful and right for you and some will not.

My final words of wisdom are these. Love everyone, including yourself. Always do the right thing, even when no one is looking. When you make mistakes, fix them and keep moving forward. Be a positive influence and role model for others. Be kind. Serve others.

Do you remember that time when we were stuck in horrible traffic when you were in college and were very late for something and I was "negative" about the situation? Do you remember what you said? You said, "Dad, we are right where we are supposed to be." I have never forgotten that phrase. I have shared it with many people and it helps me from time to time when I am not where I want to be physically or metaphorically. You have a purpose for being where you are today. You are a person of significance. All you have to do is realize that you don't know what you don't know and you need to keep learning and loving.

My pet peeves and why

- Reply to All when appropriate: If you are aware and pay attention, you will know when that is.

- Email signature on replies: If you don't have your email setup to do this and someone sends you an email that you reply to, how will they know how to contact you?

- Don't cross the line: Practice awareness and mindfulness at traffic lights and stop signs. And, don't be negative when others cross the line. It's not their fault. They haven't read this book.

- Not replacing the weights at the gym: This is an opportunity to practice being considerate of others and do the right thing. Again, don't think or speak negatively about those who don't put them back. As a matter of fact, consider returning their weights for them now and then.

What does this even mean?

I am not going to give you the answers to these, but have fun giving them a little thought. Some may be obvious, some may not be so obvious, and some you may have never heard of before.

- More than you can shake a stick at
- A bird in the hand is worth two in the bush
- A penny wise, pound foolish
- More than one way to skin a cat
- On their last leg

Things my dad said

- It might rain: When I was a young man and wanted to put off cutting the grass until tomorrow, he would often say, you may want to do it today because it may rain tomorrow. Over time, he was right so many times that it turned into an expression we both used about everything in life and the "rain" became symbolic of "things" happening that get in the way. If you put something off, something may come up that makes you wish you had done it when you had the chance. He and I used this until he passed away and I still use it today.

- Plug your brain in: This was my dad's way of saying think, be aware, and pay attention. This one has stuck with me all my life. When I forget to do something or when I make a mistake because I was careless, saying to myself, "I didn't have my brain plugged in," is my way to recognizing the root of the problem, but at the same time being a little funny and upbeat. I have talked a lot about being aware, paying attention, and being mindful, and how this affects success and happiness. To be truly successful and happy, you must keep your brain plugged in.

The impact my mom had on me

My mom passed and is no longer with us. She was the perfect mom. I hope everyone who reads this book is able to feel the same way about their mom. I don't remember anything cleaver my mom often said, but I do remember this about her. She served others. She served everyone. She did it with a smile on her face and love in her heart. I miss my mom and my dad every day. Not only would I not be here without them, but I would not be who I am without their support and influence.

Key Takeaways

- You can't do it all.

- Improve your strengths.

- Do the dreaded things first.

- Rest to recharge.

- Have hobbies.

- Decide what makes you happy and one hint, it's not money.

- When no passion, pray, rest, and take action.

- Create adventure.

- Love everyone.

- Don't worry at night.

- Relax.

- You are the average of the five people you spend the most time with.

- Associate with positive, successful, happy people.

- Be authentic. Be yourself. You can be you better than anyone else on the planet.

- How to make a decision - Think in the future.

- Repetition and consistency is key to learning.

- Because we have always done it that way - turkey story

- Use "and" rather than "but"

- Find a few friends to hold you accountable for positive talk.

- It's ok to say, "Let me take some time to give that some thought."

- Go change the world!

- You can do this!

Action Steps

- Make a list of the five people you spend the most time with. Are there others that you would like to move to the top five and switch with someone who is there now?

- Make a list of your current hobbies. Make a list of hobbies you have had in the past. Make a list of hobbies you think might enjoy. Now, create one list from those three that will be your new current hobby list for this year.

- Go change the world!
- You can do this!

Suggested Reading

- The Go-Giver by Bob Burg and John David Mann

- The 80/20 Principle by Richard Koch

- The E-Myth Revisited by Michael E. Gerber

- The eMyth Insurance Store by Michael E. Gerber and John K. Rost

- Profit First by Mike Michalowicz

- Built to Sell by John Warrillow

Favorite Quote

- The best time to plant a tree is twenty years ago. The second best time is today.

References

Blanchard, Ken, and Sheldon Bowles. *High Five!: the Magic of Working Together.* HarperCollins Business, 2001.

Blanchard, Kenneth H., and Sheldon M. Bowles. *Gung Ho!* Morrow, 1998.

Blanchard, Kenneth H., and Spencer Johnson. *The One Minute Manager.* William Morrow an Imprint of HarperCollins Publishers, 2015.

Blanchard, Kenneth H., et al. *Customer Mania!: It's Never Too Late to Build a Customer-Focused Company.* Free Press, 2016.

Blanchard, Kenneth H., et al. *The One Minute Manager Builds High Performing Teams.* Thorsons, 2017.

Burg, Bob, and John David Mann. *The Go-Giver: a Little Story about a Powerful Business Idea.* Portfolio Penguin, 2015.

Carnegie, Dale. *How to Win Friends and Influnce People.* Embassy Books, 2018.

Gerber, Michael E. *The E-Myth Revisited: Why Most Small Businesses Don't Work and What to Do about It.* HarperCollins e-Books, 2017.

Gerber, Michael E., and John K. Rost. *The E-Myth Insurance Store Why Most Insurance Businesses Don't Work and What to Do about It.* Prodigy Business, 2013.

Holmes, Chet. *Ultimate Sales Machine: Turbocharge Your Business with Relentless Focus on 12 Key Strategies.* Portfolio Penguin, 2015.

Hsieh, Tony. *Delivering Happiness: a Path to Profits, Passion, and Purpose*. Grand Central Pub., 2013.

Koch, Richard. *80/20 Principle*. Nicholas Brealey Pub, 2017.

Maxwell, John C. *Leadership 101*. Thomas Nelson, 2002.

Michalowicz, Mike. *Profit First: Transform Any Business from a Cash-Eating Monster to a Money-Making Machine*. Portfolio/Penguin, 2017.

Port, Michael. *Book Yourself Solid: the Fastest, Easiest, and Most Reliable System for Getting More Clients than You Can Handle Even If You Hate Marketing and Selling*. Wiley, 2018.

Rackham, Neil. *SPIN-Selling*. Routledge, 2017.

Ross, Aaron, and Marylou Tyler. *Predictable Revenue: Turn Your Business into a Sales Machine with the $100 Million Best Practices of Salesforce.com*. Aaron Ross, 2012.

Ross, Aaron. *CEOFlow: Turn Your Employees into Mini-CEOs*. PebbleStorm, Inc., 2009.

Tracy, Brian. *Advanced Selling Strategies: the Proven System of Sales Ideas, Methods, and Techniques Used by Top Salespeople Everywhere*. Simon & Schuster, 1996.

Warrillow, John. *Built to Sell: Creating a Business That Can Thrive without You*. Portfolio/Penguin, 2012.

Ziglar, Zig. *Sell Your Way to the Top*. Simon & Schuster Audio, 1994.

Index

www.ingramcontent.com/pod-product-compliance
Lightning Source LLC
Chambersburg PA
CBHW061325220326
41599CB00026B/5034